3.00

Lola

D1293510

Your Hope of Glory

The Life and Teachings of Jesus

ELIZABETH SAND TURNER

UNITY SCHOOL OF CHRISTIANITY
UNITY VILLAGE, MISSOURI 64063

Your Hope of Glory
was first published in 1959.

Lovingly Dedicated to

CHARLES FILLMORE

who helped untold numbers to find
in the Master's teachings "the food
which abideth unto eternal life."

FOREWORD

What is the secret of Jesus' enduring influence? One basic reason is that man is a spiritual being, made in the image and likeness of God. Everyone may not be aware of this, but we instinctively respond to the One whose every word and act was evidence of His divinity. The voice of our divine self may be faint; we may even deliberately close our ears to it, yet it continues to sound and ever urges a climb to higher ground. Jesus made this ascent, and by our spiritual kinship with Him we are drawn to Him. Charles Fillmore says:

We are all in mind related to a great creative Spirit that infuses its very life into our mind and body when we turn our attention to it. We have mentally wandered away from this creative Spirit or Father-Mind and lost contact with its life-giving currents. Jesus made connection for us, and through Him we again begin to draw vitality from the great fountainhead (JC 4).

For hundreds of years Hebrew seers had believed that a man was to come who would fulfill the noblest ideals of humanity. This ideal man, they foretold, would be the Messiah, the anointed One, the beloved of God, the Saviour. They prophesied that He would lead His people out of darkness and distress into light and joy. From the days of Moses, who declared, "Jehovah thy God will raise up unto thee a prophet from the midst of thee, of thy brethren, like unto me; unto him ye shall hearken" (Deut. 18:15),

5

throughout the period of the great literary prophets, there had been these predictions. How and when this Messiah was to come the prophets did not know; nevertheless, they had a definite conception of what He would be like. Of all the prophets, Isaiah had the clearest vision. He said that a maiden would bear a son whose name would be Immanuel (which means God with us). He would be a redeemer, a king to whose sovereignty there would be no end:

The people that walked in darkness have seen a great light: they that dwelt in the land of the shadow of death, upon them hath the light shined. . . . For unto us a child is born, unto us a son is given; and the government shall be upon his shoulder: and his name shall be called Wonderful, Counsellor, Mighty God, Everlasting Father, Prince of Peace (Isa. 9:2-5).

Isaiah gave a lucid description of the nature of the anointed One:

The Spirit of Jehovah shall rest upon him, the spirit of wisdom and understanding, the spirit of counsel and might, the spirit of knowledge and of the fear of Jehovah. . . . and he shall not judge after the sight of his eyes, neither decide after the hearing of his ears; but with righteousness shall he judge the poor, and decide with equity for the meek of the earth; and he shall smite the earth with the rod of his mouth; and with the breath of his lips shall he slay the wicked. And righteousness shall be the girdle of his waist, and faithfulness the girdle of his loins (Isa. 11:2-5).

The prophet declared that the kingdom of the Messiah would be universal, not only for man but for all creation:

6

And the wolf shall dwell with the lamb, and the leopard shall lie down with the kid; and the calf and the young lion and the fatling together; and a little child shall lead them. . . . They shall not hurt nor destroy in all my holy mountain; for the earth shall be full of the knowledge of Jehovah, as the waters cover the sea (Isa. 11:6-9).

Finally there came into the world the One who was to fulfill these great prophecies to the utmost— Jesus of Nazareth, who is Christ the Saviour. Christ, from the Greek word *christos,* has the same meaning as the Hebrew word for Messiah.

According to the Unity teachings the name Jesus Christ has a twofold meaning that should be clearly understood before you read farther. Jesus was the man of Galilee. Christ is the perfect spiritual self of every man. Charles Fillmore states:

Jesus represents God's idea of man in expression; Christ is that idea in the absolute. Jesus Christ was the type man, which includes all the mental phases through which man passes in demonstrating life's problems. So we find Jesus Christ passing through all the trials and temptations and mental variations of each of us, "yet without sin," that is, not falling under the dominion of evil thoughts (MD 345).

Unity believes that in the Gospels a spiritual meaning underlies characters and events. Jesus represents spiritual man in activity. He is the outpicturing of the potential spiritual self that abides in each of us. His life therefore typifies stages in our own unfoldment. The apostles represent the twelve spiritual faculties or powers that are to be brought forth in our life. The Pharisees and Sadducees stand for qualities in the human consciousness that oppose or resist the Christ and should be eliminated.

Our real nature is like that of Jesus, for did He not say, "Ye are the light of the world" (Matt. 5:14), and bid us to let our light shine? He said also, "He that believeth on me, the works that I do shall he do also; and greater *works* than these shall he do" (John 14:12). We have indeed borne "the image of the earthy" (I Cor. 15:49); that is, through ignorance of our divine self we have functioned on a lower or earthy plane of consciousness; but, as Paul foresaw, "we shall also bear the image of the heavenly" (I Cor. 15:49). This higher state of consciousness is possible to all who follow Jesus and claim their divine heritage. His promise is, "I go to prepare a place for you. . . . that where I am, *there* ye may be also" (John 14:2, 3). Through His great overcoming Jesus released the Christ consciousness into the universal ethers, and those who keep His word may enter into it. Jesus, therefore, is our Way-Shower and only Saviour. Very often when we think of our Saviour, we recall the words that Charles Fillmore proclaimed the greatest words ever spoken: "Christ in you, the hope of glory" (Col. 1:27).

The material contained in this book covers the life and teachings of Jesus as interpreted by the Unity School of Christianity and is based on the chronological sequence given in "A Harmony of the Gospels," by A. T. Robertson, published by Harper and Brothers, New York City.

The four Gospels, Matthew, Mark, Luke, and

8

John, are biographies of Jesus. Each presents a portrait of this Man among men. Mark's Gospel, the first to be recorded, was written between A.D. 65 and 75 and is the shortest of the four. Apparently, little thought was given to the arrangement of material; yet, the writing is simple, clear, and vivid. The author, John Mark, accompanied Peter during the latter's missionary work in Rome, and he wrote of Jesus as Peter described Him. Through his words one pictures Jesus as the divine worker rather than as the Teacher, and feels the energy and intense activity with which Jesus performed His ministry.

The Gospel of Matthew was written in the decade between A.D. 80 and 90, and endeavored to prove that Jesus was the Messiah of Jewish prophecy as well as the King of all men. Matthew's Gospel is the longest of the four and contains practically all information that is found in Mark's Gospel. Because of its effective grouping of the teachings of Jesus, notably those contained in the Sermon on the Mount, this Gospel precedes the other three in the Christian canon.

Luke's Gospel was written only a few years after the Gospel of Matthew. The writing incorporates much of Mark's Gospel, but it has more continuity than the earlier two and is considered superior from a literary standpoint. Luke, a physician by profession, was a convert of Paul's and became his companion on missionary journeys. His writing reveals Jesus to the Gentile world as the Great Physician who healed the souls and bodies of men.

The last of the Gospels was written by John toward the end of the first century A.D. Evidently he was acquainted with the three former Gospels, and though he relates the major events as given in the Synoptic Gospels, Matthew, Mark, and Luke, he records many not known to them. His account begins not with the human Jesus, but with the divine Word, the same that was "in the beginning with God." He recounts fewer miracles and parables, but dwells more on the teaching of Jesus in the great Discourses, constantly picturing Jesus as the Son of God come to earth. His Gospel touches profound depths of spirituality, rounding out and adding to the portrait of Jesus as given by Matthew, Mark, and Luke.

Each of the four writers tells of Jesus' wondrous deeds of mercy, His love for the Father and His fellow men, His miracles, and finally of His crucifixion. Each tells of the glory of Easter morn and of His appearances after the Resurrection. Each emphasizes His greatness and also His nearness to those who believe.

Jesus is the most sublime character the world has known. He continues to hold a paramount place in the lives of men, and hence in the affairs of the world. Those who accept Him and trust Him find a new and finer side of themselves coming into expression, a side they did not know they possessed. They discover that peace of mind is not something to be wished for, but something that is attained. They feel a love that makes God a reality and enables them to see Him in their fellow men. They detect in themselves a capacity to accomplish far beyond their former expectations. Not only individuals but countries that profess Christianity rise or fall in proportion to their ability to live according to the teachings of the Master. By understanding His life and following His teachings we may find salvation from all mortal limitation and do our part to bring the kingdom of All-Good to earth.

As we learn to take the steps in consciousness that Jesus taught, we discover that we are walking a better way, learning Truth, living happier and more useful lives. We are accepting the challenge proffered by Paul, "be renewed in the spirit of your mind." And imperceptibly, perhaps, yet very surely, we are actually putting on the "new man, that after God hath been created in righteousness and holiness of truth" (Eph. 4:24).

As you read the Master's majestic and inspiring words, may you feel His love poured out upon you and His power quickening your whole being. Then you too shall say with the Roman centurion and others who watched at the Cross, "Truly this was the Son of God" (Matt. 27:54). Even as you make this acknowledgment, there shall come quickly to you His reassuring promise, "Lo, I am with you always, even unto the end of the world" (Matt. 28:20).

Elizabeth Sand Turner

11

PUBLISHER'S NOTE

The sources of quotations from the writings of Charles Fillmore are indicated by the following initials, each of which refers to a particular book:

ASP Atom-Smashing Power of Mind

CH   Christian Healing

JC   Jesus Christ Heals

KL   Keep a True Lent

MD   Metaphysical Bible Dictionary

MG   Mysteries of Genesis

MJ   Mysteries of John

P   Prosperity

TM   The Twelve Powers of Man

TP   Teach Us to Pray

TT   Talks on Truth

Bible references are given in the usual way (Matt. 1:1). References to other books are given in full.

Unless otherwise noted, Bible quotations are from the American Standard Version.

CONTENTS

CHAPTER I

The Saviour Is Born

And there were shepherds in the same country abiding in the fields, and keeping watch by night over their flock. And an angel of the Lord stood by them, and the glory of the Lord shone round about them: and they were sore afraid. And the angel said unto them, Be not afraid; for behold, I bring you good tidings of great joy which shall be to all the people: for there is born to you this day in the city of David a Saviour, who is Christ the Lord. And this is *the sign unto you: Ye shall find a babe wrapped in swaddling clothes and lying in a manger. And suddenly there was with the angel a multitude of the heavenly host praising God, and saying,*

> *Glory to God in the highest,*
> *And on earth peace among men*
> *in whom he is well pleased.*

I N THESE IMMORTAL WORDS the Bible records the most momentous event in the history of mankind—the birth of Jesus. In 4 B.C., or near that time, there lived in the village of Nazareth of Galilee a Jew whose name was Joseph. He was a carpenter by trade, but the blood of Israel's kings flowed in his veins, for Joseph could trace his lineage back to David, the greatest of the Hebrew monarchs. Joseph was a kindly man and deeply religious. His family had originated in Bethlehem, but for some years Joseph had lived in Nazareth, where he became betrothed to Mary, a young Jewess of royal

15

descent, and even more pious than Joseph. Tradition claims that Joseph was a widower and many years Mary's senior.

The New Testament gives very little information regarding Mary, but the Apocryphal Gospels are full of stories connected with her. These stories state that she was born to aged and childless parents, Joachim and Anna; that at the age of three she was dedicated to God at the Temple, and remained there until she was twelve, so increasing in virtue that angels ministered unto her; that as a young maiden she was betrothed to Joseph, who had been selected for her by a miraculous sign.

There are two accounts in the Gospels relating events immediately preceding the marriage of Joseph and Mary. Luke records the annunciation to Mary:

Now in the sixth month the angel Gabriel was sent from God unto a city of Galilee, named Nazareth, to a virgin betrothed to a man whose name was Joseph, of the house of David; and the virgin's name was Mary. And he came in unto her, and said, Hail, thou that art highly favored, the Lord *is* with thee. But she was greatly troubled at the saying, and cast in her mind what manner of salutation this might be. And the angel said unto her, Fear not, Mary: for thou hast found favor with God. And behold, thou shalt conceive in thy womb, and bring forth a son, and shalt call his name JESUS. He shall be great, and shall be called the Son of the Most High: and the Lord God shall give unto him the throne of his father David: and he shall reign over the house of Jacob for ever; and of his kingdom there shall be no end. And Mary said unto the angel, How shall this be, seeing I know not a man? And the angel answered and said unto her, The Holy Spirit shall come unto thee, and the power of the Most High shall overshadow thee: wherefore also the holy thing which is begotten shall be called the Son of God (Luke 1:26-35).

Mary represents "the soul that magnifies the Lord 'daily in the temple' and through its devotion prepares itself for the higher life" (MD 427).

Because writers on spiritual subjects are not in complete agreement on their definition of the word *soul*, it is well to explain Unity's teaching as regards the threefold nature of man as Spirit, soul, and body:

Spirit is I AM (Christ) the same in character as Divine Mind, or God. Soul is man's consciousness—that which he has apprehended or developed out of Spirit; also the impressions that he has received from the outer world. Soul is both conscious and subconscious. Body is the form of both Spirit and soul (MD 628).

In the Unity teaching the word *soul* is generally used to designate the total consciousness, but in Bible interpretation as given by Charles Fillmore, men represent that phase of the soul we term mind, and women represent the emotional or feeling nature of the soul.

Mary symbolizes the purified soul that has become highly intuitive and sensitive to inspiration from the Lord. To the soul in this state, an angel (spiritual thought) comes: "Hail, thou that are highly favored, the Lord is with thee."

We are confused when we first receive spiritual inspiration. (Mary was "troubled at the saying, and cast in her mind what manner of salutation this

might be"). In the initial stage of our spiritual awakening, we are not aware of what is happening. It is
different from any experience we have ever had. If
we will be still, a reassurance will come: "Fear not,
Mary: for thou hast found favor with God. And behold, thou shalt . . . bring forth a son . . . He shall
be great, and shall be called the Son of the Most
High," that is, we are to be receptacles for the outpouring of Spirit; we are to bring good into visible
form. But how can this be? It is not in accord with
the human laws with which we are familiar.

And the angel answered and said unto her, The Holy
Spirit shall come upon thee, and the power of the Most
High shall overshadow thee; wherefore also the holy thing
which is begotten shall be called the Son of God (Luke
1:35).

Mary had become purified by spiritual aspiration
and dedicated to the will of God. She was highly intuitive and thus receptive to a revelation from the
Holy Spirit, and was aware of the quickening of new
life. The idea of perfect man (Christ) was immacu-
lately or spiritually conceived by her. This idea, filled
with the life and wisdom of Spirit, was gradually to
form its outer vehicle of expression, Jesus.

When a person's soul attains the degree of spiritual unfoldment represented by Mary, the "power
of the Most High" overshadows it and there is conceived in the consciousness the idea of the indwelling
Christ. This is "the holy thing which is begotten" not
of the human but of the divine, and "shall be called

the Son of God." One's whole being is animated
and vitalized by the outpouring of life from on high.
Even as any idea that is dominant in consciousness
comes into manifestation in time, so does this greatest of all ideas find embodiment in the changed life
of the individual. His words and his deeds express
the Christ as did those of Jesus. Thus, the circumstances of Jesus' conception and virgin birth have
great meaning for those who aspire to spiritual attainment:

Unity accepts the virgin birth of Jesus, and finds in
it a deep metaphysical significance. Though the virgin birth
is considered a miraculous event, the Truth student should
remember that the way of spiritual law transcends material
law. "The things which are impossible with men are possible with God."

Tradition tells us that Mary was not only virgin by
reason of her unmarried state, but she was also virgin in
mind and heart. We believe this has a symbolic meaning.
Just as Jesus was born to one whose mind and heart were
pure and uncorrupted, so too is the Spirit of Christ born
into individual consciousness as the mind and heart are
made pure and clean, freed of all mortal thought and sin.

No one should feel that the manner of Jesus' birth made
Him so different from the rest of mankind that we all cannot be perfect as He was perfect. It was Jesus' divine origin
that gave Him power, not the peculiar circumstances surrounding His physical birth. Each individual, though he
may be unaware of it, is a divine child of God, heir to all
of God's goodness. Each bears the same relationship to
God as Jesus: all are equally sons and children of the Most
High (Pamphlet—*The New Birth*).

In the process of bringing a spiritual realization

into manifestation, there is involved yet another faculty of the mind. Joseph, betrothed to Mary, represents the understanding. We receive the idea of the indwelling Christ when the soul (Mary) becomes sensitized to Spirit; but this revelation must be protected and sustained by the understanding (Joseph). Even as Mary was at first troubled by the angel's announcement that she would bear a son, so, too, was Joseph. "And Joseph being a righteous man, and not willing to make her a public example, was minded to put her away privily" (Matt. 1:19). His intention to put Mary away "means that we do not in the first stages of the birth of Christ in us understand the process, and sometimes are moved to put it away from us" (MD 367).

But when he [Joseph] thought on these things, behold, an angel of the Lord appeared to him in a dream, saying, Joseph, thou son of David, fear not to take unto thee Mary thy wife: for that which is conceived in her is of the Holy Spirit. And she shall bring forth a son; and thou shalt call his name JESUS; for it is he that shall save his people from their sins (Matt. 1:20-22).

Mary received a revelation from the Lord when the angel appeared to her, but Joseph received his revelation indirectly—the angel appeared to him in a dream. This signifies that spiritual enlightenment comes more directly through intuition than through understanding. However, when the understanding is illumined, it is obedient to divine guidance. Joseph acted on the inspiration he received and devotedly cared for Mary.

Mary was aware of the divine life she carried. Desiring some time for quiet and meditation, she went to the hill country to visit her cousin Elisabeth. Her devout and exalted frame of mind are expressed in the beautiful prayer of praise that has come to be known as the Magnificat:

"My soul doth magnify the Lord,
  And my spirit hath rejoiced in God my Saviour. . . .
  For he that is mighty hath done to me great things;
  And holy is his name" (Luke 1:46-49).

Such a state of exaltation nurtures the divine idea that has been quickened in the consciousness. Mary believed "in the so-called miraculous as a possibility. She expected the birth of the Messiah, according to the promise of the Holy Spirit" (MD 428).

It is only when we have been awakened to a realization of the divine life (Christ) in us that we are ready to give attention to the steps which must be taken in consciousness in order to express outwardly that which has been conceived inwardly. In the life of Jesus these steps are shown by His teachings, His healings, and His final overcoming. Jesus is spiritual man made manifest. Through Him we discover the way of salvation. "It is he that shall save his people from their sins" (Matt. 1:22).

Paul admonishes us, "have this mind in you, which was also in Christ Jesus." We should study this Mind in order to emulate it. Jesus is the pattern. He is the example for all who would come into spiritual consciousness and express the Christ or divine self.

As the account of the life of Jesus is continued, it should be with the understanding that we are witnessing the unfolding of our own consciousness Godward. The events of His life are different from those we encounter in our life, but the underlying principle is the same. In perceiving this, we can read of these events not only as happening to one man nearly two thousand years ago, but also as stages in our own spiritual progress.

Shortly before Jesus' birth a decree was sent out by the Roman government that each Jew should enroll for taxation in his native city. As Joseph was of the lineage of David, it was necessary for him to go to Bethlehem for enrollment. Not wishing to leave Mary alone in Nazareth, Joseph took her with him on the journey:

And it came to pass, while they were there, the days were fulfilled that she should be delivered. And she brought forth her firstborn son; and she wrapped him in swaddling clothes and laid him in a manger, because there was no room for them in the inn (Luke. 2:6, 7).

Bethlehem means "house of bread" and signifies divine substance. Substance is the spiritual essence that underlies all manifest form. The soul (Mary), heavily charged with the divine idea, had to be unified with substance before there could be a manifestation. But "in the inn" there is no room for the divine idea to come forth. The inn symbolizes both the human, worldly habitat and interest that has no place for spiritual things. Mary was the channel or vehicle for the expression of the Christ; but the birth had to be brought about in simplicity and quietness. This simplicity and quietness is symbolized in the fact that Jesus' birth took place in a cave or grotto where animals were kept.

The shepherds, who were the first to pay homage to the infant Jesus, represent those who have faith in God. To such persons illumination comes as "an angel" with the glad tidings that Christ the Saviour is born. When we are obedient to the revelation and put forth effort to "see this thing that is come to pass" (Luke 2:15), we find that the Christ is no longer a hope, but a reality. We then praise God for His life, which is manifested in our midst every day.

The shepherds told Mary and Joseph all that had occurred, and Mary "kept all these sayings, pondering them in her heart" (Luke 2:19). In the depths of our being, the expression of divine life is sacred and not to be discussed promiscuously. We meditate on it, guard it, and revere it.

On the eighth day after His birth Jesus was circumcised, according to the Jewish custom. The word *circumcision* means "cutting off," and to the Jews it symbolized a cutting off of the sins of the human personality and the dedication of the child to God. In the life of Jesus this law was fulfilled early, even as He later voluntarily fulfilled the law in every respect. However, in His life an additional significance is given to circumcision, even as it is to baptism and the keeping of the Sabbath:

Under the law of Jesus Christ, circumcision is fulfilled in its spiritual meaning—the purification of the individual from the law of sin and death. One is circumcised in the true inner significance of the word only by being thoroughly purified in soul. Then the glory of the inner soul cleansing and purifying works out into the outer consciousness and the body and sets one free from all sensual, corruptible thoughts and activities (MD 152).

The Mosaic law required each Jewish mother to have a period of purification after the birth of a child, a period of forty days in the case of a male child. After this, in order to complete her purification the mother must offer a year-old lamb and a young pigeon or turtledove, though persons in poorer circumstances might substitute another pigeon or turtledove for the lamb (Lev. 12). In order to comply with this law and the further requirement of presenting their son to the Lord, Mary and Joseph took Jesus to the Temple in Jerusalem. There Simeon, an aged priest, and Anna, a prophetess, met them and recognized Jesus as the promised Messiah. Simeon had received a promise from the Lord that he should not die until he had beheld the Saviour. After he took the Child in his arms and praised God, Simeon said:

Now lettest thou thy servant depart, Lord,
According to thy word, in peace;
For mine eyes have seen thy salvation,
Which thou hast prepared before the face of all peoples;
A light for revelation to the Gentiles,
And the glory of thy people Israel (Luke 2:29-32).

Simeon symbolizes "one who listens and obeys. Hearing, in its higher aspect, refers to the state of mind in the devout Christian that looks for and expects spiritual guidance and instruction direct from God. It may be summed up in the word 'receptivity.' This new consciousness of the indwelling immortal life takes the place of hope, expectancy, obedience" (MD 619).

The good news of the birth of the Saviour had also reached the Wise Men. They had seen a star in the heavens, which to them meant that one had been born who would be "King of the Jews." Journeying to Jerusalem, they inquired of Herod the Great where they might find the new King.

The Wise Men from the east represent:

The stored-up resources of the soul, which rise to the surface when its depths are stirred by a great spiritual revelation. They are the inner realms of consciousness that, like books of life, have kept the records of past lives and held them in reserve for the great day when the soul would receive the supreme ego, Jesus. These "Wise-Men" represent the wisdom that is carried within the soul from previous incarnations. The east represents the within, man's inner consciousness (MD 677).

Now Herod, knowing of the prophecies that there would come a Messiah, was greatly disturbed by the Wise Men's inquiry. He had been appointed king of the Jews by the Roman emperor in 40 B.C., and was well aware of the hatred the Jews held for him, for he was a foreigner and a symbol of their

subjection to Rome. Herod, in turn, despised his subjects and was oppressive and often cruel in his treat-
ment of them. Realizing that his throne might be in
jeopardy, he called together the chief priests and
scribes, and asked where their scriptures predicted
the Messiah would be born. Upon being informed
that Bethlehem was the place foretold, Herod sent
the Wise Men there with instructions to return to
him when they had found the Child, so that he, too,
might worship Him. However, his real intent was to
have the Babe slain.

And they, having heard the king, went their way; and
lo, the star, which they saw in the east, went before them,
till it came and stood over where the young child was.
And when they saw the star, they rejoiced with exceeding
great joy. And they came into the house and saw the young
child with Mary his mother; and they fell down and
worshipped him; and opening their treasures they offered
unto him gifts, gold and frankincense and myrrh (Matt.
2:9-11).

The gifts of the Magi represent "the inner resources of Spirit, which are open to the Christ Mind.
Gold represents the riches of Spirit; frankincense,
the beauty of Spirit; myrrh, the eternity of Spirit"
(MD 677).

Herod signifies "the ruling will of the physical,
the ego in the sense consciousness" (MD 274). This
will ever seeks to destroy that which is spiritual, because it sees in the things of Spirit a power that
threatens its rule.

The Wise Men were warned in a dream not to

return to Jerusalem, so they "departed into their own country another way." Herod, failing to receive a report from the Wise Men, became exceedingly fearful. In an effort to make secure his throne, he issued an edict that all male children under two years of age, living in Bethlehem or the surrounding country, should be put to death. Herod, however, did not accomplish his purpose, for Joseph (understanding) was warned in a dream to flee into Egypt with Mary and Jesus.

Egypt typifies the sense place of thought that temporarily harbors the Christ. After Joseph spent a period of time there, he was divinely guided to leave and return to his native land. Herod The Great had died, and his son Archelaus reigned. When Joseph heard this, he did not go to Jerusalem, "and being warned *of God* in a dream, he withdrew into the parts of Galilee, and came and dwelt in a city called Nazareth" (Matt. 2:22, 23). The return to Nazareth was necessary, for Nazareth represents "the commonplace mind of man, but it is a place of development through which the Christ comes into expression" (MD 473).

CHAPTER II

The Voice in the Wilderness

*And the child grew, and waxed strong, filled with
wisdom: and the grace of God was upon him.*

WHEN JESUS had completed His twelfth year
He was allowed to accompany Mary and
Joseph from their home in Nazareth to the
Holy City for the observance of the great Feast of
the Passover. At this age a Jewish boy became a "son
of the Law," a status that implied spiritual responsibility, and we find Jesus attending His first
passover to discharge this responsibility.

We can imagine how strange and vastly interesting to the Nazarene lad was His first journey to
Jerusalem, a distance of approximately eighty miles.
As was the custom in those days, Jesus and His parents joined a group of Galilean pilgrims and, together, the band made its way slowly south through
Samaria to Judea, a journey of four or five days.

The city of Jerusalem was teeming with visitors
from many parts of Palestine and from various countries in the Mediterranean area, for Jewish pilgrims
and proselytes came yearly to the Temple for celebration of the great feasts, of which there were several. Notable among them were the Passover, the
Feast of Tabernacles, and the Feast of the Dedication. In this particular instance the crowds were
drawn to the city on the occasion of the Feast of
the Passover. This feast commemorated the de-

liverance of the Jews from Egyptian bondage under the leadership of Moses.

The observance of the Feast of the Passover lasted a week. When the ceremonials were over, the Galilean caravan started homeward. It is understandable that in such a large group a boy might easily be lost sight of, and Mary and Joseph did not notice Jesus' absence until they had gone a day's journey. We can imagine their dismay when their inquiries among kinsmen and acquaintances failed to disclose His whereabouts. Hastily they returned to Jerusalem to seek Him:

And it came to pass, after three days they found him in the temple, sitting in the midst of the teachers, both hearing them, and asking them questions: and all that heard him were amazed at his understanding and his answers. And when they saw him, they were astonished: and his mother said unto him, Son, why hast thou thus dealt with us? behold, thy father and I sought thee sorrowing. And he said unto them, How is it that ye sought me? knew ye not that I must be in my Father's house? And they understood not the saying which he spake unto them (Luke 2:46-50).

This was Jesus' first announcement of His dedication to God's service. He had reached the age of twelve, and this number, spiritually interpreted, signifies completeness or wholeness. We have attained the first stage of spiritual maturity when we understand and acknowledge that we must be in our "Father's house" or "about my Father's business" as the Authorized Version of the Bible gives it. It

should be our vital concern to learn God's law, to
express His qualities that are latent within us, and
to do His work.

And he went down with them, and came to Nazareth;
and he was subject unto them: and his mother kept all
these sayings in her heart.

And Jesus advanced in wisdom and stature, and in
favor with God and men (Luke 2:51, 52).

All great leaders have periods of preparation for
the work they are to do. This is especially true of
one who sets himself to serve God. No doubt the
eighteen years that followed Jesus' appearance in the
Temple served as a time of inward preparation for
Him.

All Jewish boys were taught a trade. And Jesus
learned carpentry from Joseph. Joseph is not mentioned after Jesus began His ministry, and it is assumed that he died before this time. Possibly, Jesus
took Joseph's place as head of the family. In addition to His work, however, He must have spent
many hours in study, meditation, and prayer. No one
advances in "wisdom and stature" without using
his time to advantage. There have been many specu-
lations as to Jesus' activity during the so-called "silent years" of His life, but the Gospels, the only re-
liable record, indicate that He spent them unevent-
fully in the little village of Nazareth. Charles Fillmore says:

Jesus was imbued with a spirit purely His own. He did
not borrow His mission, or His words, or His precepts

from Egypt, Persia, or India. He was a genius that burned with His own wick and oil (TT 67).

At the age of thirty Jesus left Nazareth and journeyed to the place on the banks of the Jordan River in Judea where John the Baptist was preaching and baptizing.

John formed the connecting link between Judaism and Christianity by his recognition of Jesus as the Messiah long promised by Hebrew prophecy. His mission was to prepare the Jews for Jesus' message, and this he did with all the ardor of the reformer that he was.

"I am the voice of one crying in the wilderness, Make straight the way of the Lord" (John 1:23), cried this great forerunner of Jesus.

From the standpoint of spiritual interpretation John the Baptist plays an essential role. He represents the illumined intellect; that is, the mind turned toward spiritual things. The mind can function on various levels of consciousness. When a person is concerned exclusively with worldly considerations, his mentality expresses on the lowest or sense level. As he progresses mentally, the more intangible values of life command his attention. The faculties of reason and judgment develop and gradually supersede more instinctual desires. Moving still higher in mental development, he becomes aware of the existence of a spiritual realm and longs to know more of it. In time spiritual concerns entirely outweigh material or purely intellectual ones, for a divine idea has il-

lumined the mind. This is the John-the-Baptist consciousness. Charles Fillmore states:

> He [John] signifies a high intellectual perception of
> Truth, but one not yet quickened of Spirit. John represents
> that attitude of mind in which we are zealous for the rule
> of Spirit. This attitude is not spiritual, but a perception of
> spiritual possibilities and an activity in making conditions
> in which Spirit may rule (MD 357).

In individual unfoldment, we begin our conscious
identification with God in that mental state symbolized by John. And even as the prophet (John)
was the forerunner of the Saviour (Jesus), so, too,
is the illumined intellect the predecessor of full spiritual realization. Thus, a study of John's life and
ministry reveals steps on our spiritual way. Only as
we understand and profit by the greatness and also
the limitations of the intellect can we move forward
toward the Christ consciousness.

John was the son of Zacharias, a priest, and
Elisabeth, elderly Jews who lived in Judea. They
had long wanted a son but it seemed that their
prayers were not to be answered. Yet one day as
Zacharias was performing his duties at the Temple
in Jerusalem,

> There appeared unto him an angel of the Lord stand-
> ing on the right side of the altar of incense. And Zacharias
> was troubled when he saw *him,* and fear fell upon him.
> But the angel said unto him, Fear not, Zacharias; because
> thy supplication is heard, and thy wife Elisabeth shall bear
> thee a son, and thou shalt call his name John. And thou
> shalt have joy and gladness; and many shall rejoice at his

birth. For he shall be great in the sight of the Lord . . . and he shall be filled with the Holy Spirit . . . and many of the children of Israel shall he turn unto the Lord their God. And he shall go before his face in the spirit and power of Elijah, to turn the hearts of the fathers to the children, and the disobedient *to walk* in the wisdom of the just; to make ready for the Lord a people prepared *for him* (Luke 1:12-17).

Metaphysically, Zacharias represents spiritual consciousness and Elisabeth signifies the soul in the feminine or love consciousness. (MD 684, 193) Together they represent the whole consciousness, thought and feeling, expressing on the spiritual plane. Hence, they were receptive to a divine idea (an angel of the Lord). Note, however, that just as we are often awed by the revelation of Spirit and find it difficult to accept, so, too, was Zacharias fearful and doubting. "Whereby shall I know this? for I am an old man, and my wife well stricken in years" (Luke 1:18). Because of his doubt Zacharias was struck dumb. The implication here is that disbelief keeps us from speaking the word that has been revealed. Zacharias was released from dumbness when John was born, and he praised and gave thanks to God:

Blessed *be* the Lord, the God of Israel;
For he hath visited and wrought redemption for his people
     (Luke 1:68).

Elisabeth, the mother of John, and Mary, the mother of Jesus, were cousins; hence, Jesus and John were related. This tells us that the intellect in its highest state is closely connected with spiritual realization, perceiving the Christ and striving to prepare the consciousness to accept the divine idea ("make ready for the Lord a people prepared *for him*").

John was less than a year younger than Jesus. Before he began his public work he lived the life of an ascetic in the Judean wilderness near the shores of the Dead Sea. In his secluded haunt John studied the words of God and gradually became convinced that the prophecies concerning a Messiah were about to be fulfilled. The Anointed One, the Messiah, was to usher in the kingdom of heaven and redeem His people from all bondage, but they must be prepared to receive and follow Him. Holiness was required of them, and in this they were sadly lacking. Among the masses there was much corruption, and hypocrisy lurked in the ranks of the religious leaders. The Baptist saw it as his duty to denounce such leaders in scathing words and to proclaim the way of righteousness.

John was about thirty years of age when he appeared on the banks of the Jordan and preached, speaking with all the vigor and authority that characterized the prophets of old. The Jews were startled, yet drawn to him. There had been no prophetic voice for several hundred years. Though the early prophets had often been persecuted by their contemporaries, later generations revered them. Now the throngs listened eagerly to the words of one whom they recognized as a man of God. From near and far they flocked to the banks of the Jordan to hear him.

Even John's appearance was significant. He wore "raiment of camel's hair, and a leathern girdle about his loins; and his food was locusts and wild honey" (Matt. 3:4). Such had been the costume of the earlier prophets, the camel's hair or sackcloth symbolizing repentance. The Mosaic law sanctioned the eating of locusts and wild honey.

The keynote of John's message was, "Repent ye, for the kingdom of heaven is at hand" (Matt. 3:2). Every Jewish heart thrilled at the words, "the kingdom of heaven is at hand," for this meant to them that the Messiah was soon to come. That John prefaced this announcement with the command, "Repent ye," made little difference to the Jews until he made it quite clear that they were in dire need of reforming and could not enter the kingdom without doing so. The illumined intellect understands that a change must take place in the individual before the kingdom can become a reality. As descendants of Abraham the Jews claimed the right to enter the kingdom of heaven to be set up by the Messiah. They were not prepared for John's command for repentance. Neither did they like his analysis of the conditions brought on by their sins. But repentance is a necessary step in the attainment of righteousness, and of one and all John demanded:

Bring forth therefore fruits worthy of repentance, and begin not to say within yourselves, We have Abraham to our father: for I say unto you, that God is able of these stones to raise up children unto Abraham (Luke 3:8).

To repent means to change one's mind. In a spiritual sense repentance is the act of turning from materialism and reaching for spiritual things. We cannot build a spiritual consciousness until we are willing to rid the mind of the beliefs and habits of thought that belong to the lower nature. John warned that only those who were willing to reform could receive the blessing of the coming kingdom. The choice was at hand:

> Even now the axe also lieth at the root of the trees; every tree therefore that bringeth not forth good fruit is hewn down, and cast into the fire (Luke 3:9).

In the Jordan, John baptized those who were willing to repent. Regarding this baptism, Charles Fillmore states:

> Water baptism symbolizes a cleansing process, the letting go of error. It is the first step in the realization of Truth. It is the process of pouring into consciousness the dissolving power of the Word, which breaks up and washes away all thoughts of materiality. . . . Water baptism indicates a letting-go attitude of thought, denial (MD 96).

Unity teaches that water baptism represents the purification of the consciousness and that actually the symbol (water) is unnecessary. Denial is the mental process of cleansing false thoughts from the mind by repudiating them. We deny anything that is not true of Spirit even though it may seem to be true from an earthly point of view. An affirmation is a statement of Truth. We first make a denial of error and, then, we affirm that which is good. Denials erase errors from the mind and affirmations establish spiritual ideas. The water baptism of John represents denial. The spiritual baptism of Jesus that was predicted by John and given the apostles after the Resurrection represents affirmation. (See Chapter XIV for spiritual baptism.)

John spoke of spiritual things with the voice of authority. This led many persons to ask him if he were the Christ, but John never failed to acknowledge the supremacy of Jesus. He said:

I indeed baptize you in water unto repentance: but he that cometh after me is mightier than I, whose shoes I am not worthy to bear; he shall baptize you in the Holy Spirit and *in* fire (Matt. 3:11).

When Jesus came to John to be baptized John said,

I have need to be baptized of thee, and comest thou to me? But Jesus answering said unto him, Suffer *it* now; for thus it becometh us to fulfil all righteousness. Then he suffereth him. And Jesus, when he was baptized, went up straightway from the water: and lo, the heavens opened unto him, and he saw the Spirit of God descending as a dove, and coming upon him; and lo, a voice out of the heavens, saying, This is my beloved Son, in whom I am well pleased (Matt. 3:14-17).

From this time, the baptism of Jesus by John, the lives of the two men were to touch on several occasions until John was slain during the latter part of the second year of Jesus' ministry. However, in

order to conclude the teaching regarding the illumined intellect (John), the remaining events of
the Baptist's life will follow in this chapter.

Shortly after the baptism John saw Jesus and
said to his disciples, "This is the son of God" (John
1:34). Later, when Jesus began His ministry in
Judea near the banks of the Jordan where John was
preaching, some of his followers reported that Jesus
was gaining more disciples than he was. The Baptist
replied:

> A man can receive nothing, except it have been given
> him from heaven. Ye yourselves bear me witness, that I
> said, I am not the Christ, but, that I am sent before him.
> He that hath the bride is the bridegroom: but the friend
> of the bridegroom, that standeth and heareth him, rejoiceth
> greatly because of the bridegroom's voice: this my joy
> therefore is made full. He must increase, but I must de-
> crease (John 3:27-30).

The illumined intellect (John) has a fourfold
task in preparing the consciousness to receive the
Christ: it declares the kingdom at hand; it counsels
repentance; it purifies the mind by means of denials (water baptism); and it points to a greater one
who is to come (the Christ).

John's limitation lay in his belief in evil as a
reality and in contending with it. He denounced the
Pharisees who came to hear his message, calling them
"offsprings of vipers" (Matt. 3:7). He rebuked
Herod Antipas, King of Galilee, for his marriage to
Herodias, his brother Philip's wife. This marriage
was in violation of the Mosaic Law to be sure, but

condemnation rarely corrects wrongdoing. Jesus admonished nonresistance to evil. The way of overcoming is through allying ourselves with God, not by fighting evil. We should learn to give good only. Did not Jesus say, "Whosoever shall smite thee on thy right cheek, turn to him the other also"? If we have a stanch faith in the power of God to right a condition, He will instruct us how to handle outer things. Under His guidance evils can be corrected in a harmonious way and for the good of all concerned. In keeping our attention on Him we may look through evil and perceive the good (God) and thus aid in bringing it into manifestation.

Herod Antipas, stung by the reproof of John, wanted to have him slain, but he feared an uprising of the people for they loved the Baptist. Finally, goaded on by his wife Herodias, the king imprisoned him in the lonely fortress at Machærus near the Dead Sea. Metaphysically, this means that the illumined intellect (John) is restricted by willful thoughts (Herod) and licentious emotions (Herodias).

John in prison represents

The intellect hemmed in, imprisoned, because of its magnifying sin and evil and condemning them. Some persons see the evil in the world as a power so formidable that it paralyzes all their efforts, and they accomplish nothing in the service of Truth (MD 358).

If we continue to acknowledge sin and struggle against it, we finally reach a point of uncertainty and doubt in consciousness. We are apt to lose faith

when outer conditions are trying, even though it has
formerly been revealed to us that Spirit is supreme
and we have declared this. This is what happened to
John. While in prison he began to doubt his own
revelation that Jesus was the promised Messiah, and
sent two of his disciples to Galilee to inquire of
Jesus, "Art thou he that cometh, or look we for another?" (Matt. 11:3). Perhaps Jesus had not done
what John expected or desired. Sometimes we pray
for and expect the outworking of a situation in a
certain way and are disappointed when our expectations are not fulfilled. Then we wonder if our spiritual prompting was genuine. Do not be confused
when moments of doubt come: ask as John did.

Jesus answered and said unto them [John's disciples],
Go and tell John the things which ye hear and see: the
blind receive their sight, and the lame walk, the lepers are
cleansed, and the deaf hear, and the dead are raised up,
and the poor have good tidings preached to them (Matt.
11:4).

Jesus did not need to say that He was the Messiah. His works bore witness of Him. He knew John
would understand that only a divine power which
moved through Him could enable Him to perform
the miracles that had been accomplished. If in our
moments of perplexity we will be still, we will receive confirmation from Christ that He is truly our
"all sufficiency in everything" (II Cor. 9:8). Each
of us has felt the Christ presence. We have seen evidences of His healing power. Yet now and then we

need the reassurance that He is with us and that His
work is being done.

Jesus knew the greatness of John, but He also
knew John's limitations, He said:

Among them that are born of women there hath not
arisen a greater than John the Baptist: yet he that is but
little in the kingdom of heaven is greater than he (Matt.
11:11).

Jesus' words mean that one who depends on and
uses his spiritual qualities even to a small extent is
nearer the kingdom (greater) than those who may
be more enlightened along intellectual lines.

John met his death by order of Herod Antipas.
The dramatic story is fully narrated in Mark 6:14-29.
At a sumptuous feast given by Herod, Herodias'
daughter (whose name was Salome, according to tradition), so pleased the king by her dance that he im-
pulsively offered to grant any wish she might make,
even to the half of his kingdom. "And she went out,
and said unto her mother, What shall I ask? And
she said, The head of John the Baptizer" (Mark
6:24). Herod immediately regretted his rash promise
but felt that he could not withdraw it before his
guests. He commanded a soldier to go to John in
prison and bring back the head of the valiant cham-
pion of righteousness. The higher thought (John)
is thus temporarily overcome by the unregenerate
emotions (Herodias), but its work of turning the
mind toward God has been accomplished. Charles
Fillmore states:

The death of John the Baptist refers to the passing away of that first enthusiasm for character reform which possesses the disciple at the earthly stage of his experience. This John-the-Baptist phase is not the permanent state of consciousness, but is to be followed by one that is permanent (MD 358).

CHAPTER III

Jesus' Ministry Begins

IN GOING TO John the Baptist for baptism, Jesus sought to identify Himself with the good that John was doing in teaching the people to repent. In stating that He wished to "fulfill all righteousness," Jesus was seeking a contact with all that John represented. John was the last prophet of the old dispensation. There should be no separation between the two, but rather a merging from the old to the new. Here Jesus clearly indicated that his teaching was not to debase the highest ideals of Judaism, but was to expand their spiritual meanings.

Whenever there is a complete cleansing of the consciousness (water baptism), a spiritual illumination follows. As Jesus emerged from the river, the Holy Spirit descended on Him "as a dove" (symbol of gentleness, peace, and new-creating life), and a voice (clear realization) came, bringing the announcement of His true identity: "This is my beloved Son, in whom I am well pleased" (Matt. 3:17).

Immediately after His baptism Jesus "was led up of the Spirit into the wilderness to be tempted of the devil" (Matt. 4:1). The attainment of a higher consciousness is generally followed by a testing period to give us opportunity to prove that we have accepted and can use the illumination received. The individual consciousness must be disciplined and tested before it can become master of the thoughts.

In the development of the Christ Mind, an entirely
new and wider set of ideas and situations has to be
met. Jesus' experiences in the wilderness are to show
us how to deal with the thoughts and desires of the
sense man, and to place them under proper dis-
cipline. It requires spiritual discernment and un-
selfish devotion to the highest Truth to meet and
overcome the temptations of the personal consciousness.

The Devil is the "adverse consciousness that has
been built up in ignorance and disregard of the divine law" (MD 346). Jesus had taken on the limitations of the flesh or sense man and was, therefore,
tempted in all points even as we are. He, too, had to
meet the errors of the race thought. And when he
had fasted forty days and forty nights, he afterward
hungered (Matt. 4:2).

Charles Fillmore states:

The forty days' fast is an all-round denial of sense
demands. In fasting, we in our thoughts live above the
material needs. We are "led up" and our appetites and
passions are for a season in such an eclipse that we think
that they will trouble us no more. But "he afterward hungered." There is a return to sense consciousness (MD 346).

Three great temptations were presented to Jesus,
and He met them within His own consciousness, even
as we must do. They are typical of the enticements
that come to us when we realize that we have access
to spiritual power. How are we going to use this
power? To benefit the personal man or for the glory

of God? Jesus is our great Teacher, and His experience shows us how these temptations should be met.

The first temptation was:

If thou art the Son of God, command that these stones become bread. But he answered and said, It is written, Man shall not live by bread alone, but by every word that proceedeth out of the mouth of God (Matt. 4:3, 4).

Is one ever justified in using spiritual power to gain material wealth, even if it is to be used for what one considers a worthy purpose? That God prospers those who trust and obey Him is attested throughout the Scriptures, but to center our whole attention on substance in the form of material supply defeats the purpose of a spiritual ministry. In addition:

The temptation to turn stones into bread illustrates the thought of ignorance that deceives people with the belief that they can satisfy the soul with materiality, without looking for the bread that comes from heaven, the Word of God. We must feed our soul with new truths daily, that we may grow in spiritual ways (MD 346).

The second temptation was:

Then the devil taketh him into the holy city; and he set him on the pinnacle of the temple, and saith unto him, If thou art the Son of God, cast thyself down: for it is written,

He shall give his angels charge concerning thee: and,

On their hands they shall bear thee up,

Lest haply thou dash thy foot against a stone.

Jesus saith unto him, Again it is written, Thou shalt
not make trial of the Lord thy God (Matt. 4:5-7).

This was a particularly subtle temptation, for
there was a belief among the Jews that the Messiah
was to appear in some spectacular manner. Had
Jesus performed a feat of this sort, He would have
called immediate attention to Himself. His desire
was to serve mankind. Would He not be entitled to
secure a following by performing a miracle? Charles
Fillmore states that this temptation "means that no
display of spiritual power for personal glory should
be made. We cannot make a display of our spiritual
power with safety" (MD 346). We should never
speak the word of healing with the thought in mind
to prove that Truth "works," or attempt to demonstrate any good for the purpose of convincing others
that it can be done.

The third temptation was:

Again, the devil taketh him unto an exceeding high
mountain, and showeth him all the kingdoms of the world,
and the glory of them; and he said unto him, All these
will I give thee, if thou wilt fall down and worship me.
Then saith Jesus unto him, Get thee hence, Satan: for it
is written, Thou shalt worship the Lord thy God, and him
only shalt thou serve (Matt. 4:8-10).

We should never allow ourselves to be under
the dominion of the personal consciousness. It
promises power that it cannot give, and to yield to
its alluring voice would pave the way for our own
destruction:

To worship the Devil is to worship personality; to live in personal consciousness and give it the substance of our life and thought. When the temptation arises in our consciousness to use our God-attained spiritual faculties and powers for the building of our personal ambitions, we should know that under the divine law there is but one worthy of our worship and service, the Lord God. To serve God we must build up spirituality in mind, body, and affairs (MD 346).

Jesus met each of the three types of temptation by speaking the word of Truth. The Christ Spirit will not permit God-power to be used for selfish ends. Jesus quoted from Deuteronomy in the Old Testament, thus showing His familiarity with these writings. It is helpful to memorize some of the favorite verses and promises that we find in the Bible. These are really affirmations of Truth, and by pondering on them our mind becomes imbued with spiritual ideas. In an hour of temptation these ideas come readily to mind. By our holding steadfastly to them the claims of the mortal are refuted. The strength of the Almighty moves through us, and we are able to rise above negative conditions.

Then the devil leaveth him; and behold, angels came and ministered unto him (Matt. 4:11).

When we realize our unity with God and know that we achieve development only through singleness of mind and heart, the Devil (personality) leaves us, and we are content to worship God only. Then "angels," which are our perceptive qualities

quickened to the higher level of Spirit, minister to
us. To gain self-understanding and self-dominion is
the work of God that every man must accomplish for
himself.

When we surmount temptations, we experience
release in mind and body and feel the peace and comfort of Spirit. The overcoming of temptation is our
own choosing. It is not the way of selfishness, even
though it may seem to be a claiming of the good
that is ours by divine right. It is the way of righteousness, and we have chosen it, since we love the Most
High.

After the years of inner preparation in Nazareth,
His baptism by John the Baptist, and His temptation
in the wilderness; Jesus was fully equipped to show
man the way to redemption. He was ready to begin
His public ministry, generally reckoned to have lasted
about three years. The number three represents the
trinity, or God as threefold in Being—Father, Son,
and Holy Spirit. Symbolically, the trinity represents
mind, idea, and expression; or thinker, thought, and
action. Man is likewise threefold as Spirit, soul, and
body. Thus, we can say that the years of Jesus' ministry signify a completed activity.

We should approach this time of Jesus' life with
the clear understanding that He represents spiritual
man in expression. The spiritual self, conceived and
brought forth by the purified soul, Mary, is now to
render its great service through the man, Jesus. In
Jesus we see the ideal man as he functions in all the
common affairs of life with the wisdom, love, and

power of God. Since we were created in the image and likeness of our Creator, it is our right and privilege to follow the great Way-Shower, first in consciousness and then in deed.

The first year of Jesus' ministry may be called "The Year of Obscurity," for during this time He was slowly coming into prominence. The events of this period are scanty. The overcoming of three temptations marked the end of Jesus' preparatory period. He then returned to the banks of the Jordan where John the Baptist was preaching. When the Baptist saw Him he said to the two disciples who were with him, "Behold, the Lamb of God!" (John 1:36). One of these disciples was Andrew, and it is thought that John was the other. These two immediately left the Baptist and followed Jesus:

And Jesus turned, and beheld them following, and saith unto them, What seek ye? And they said unto him, Rabbi . . . where abidest thou? He saith unto them, Come, and ye shall see (John 1:38, 39).

When the illumined intellect (John the Baptist) reveals the presence of spiritual man (Jesus), we are greatly interested and ask, "Where abidest thou?" Where is the habitat of the Christ? No one can tell us, not even Jesus as a man. He does, however, issue an invitation, "Come, and ye shall see." We "come" by turning in mind and heart to the things of Spirit. We want the things of Spirit, yet we are often reluctant to release worldly interests. Our desires are for both spiritual and material blessings, but the latter can be secured permanently only if we seek first the kingdom of God and His righteousness. Ours must be a willingness to leave the outer and turn to the inner. How else can we know where He lives? To follow Him ("come") is an inward, spiritual journey. If we take it, we shall discover ("see") the abiding place of the Christ.

After Andrew had contacted Jesus, he lost no time in finding his brother Simon Peter, to whom he exuberantly exclaimed, "We have found the Messiah"! (John 1:41). Immediately Simon Peter went also to Jesus, and when Jesus saw him He said, "Thou art Simon the Son of John: thou shalt be called Cephas (which is by interpretation, Peter)" (John 1:42). Jesus was quick to recognize the one who was to become His foremost apostle.

The next day Jesus returned to Galilee and went to the city of Bethsaida. There He saw Philip, a fisherman, to whom He gave the invitation, "Follow me" (John 1:43). Philip promptly sought his friend, Nathanael (called Bartholomew in the Synoptic Gospels, as this was probably Nathanael's surname), and announced, "We have found him of whom Moses in the law, and the prophets, wrote, Jesus of Nazareth, the son of Joseph" (John 1:45). Nathanael was somewhat skeptical, for Nazareth was an obscure, even an ill-reputed village, and in Nathanael's opinion it was no place for the home of the Messiah. "Can any good thing come out of Nazareth?" he asked. Philip silenced him with the words, "Come and see" (John 1:46).

Jesus saw Nathanael coming to him, and saith of him, Behold, an Israelite indeed, in whom is no guile! Nathanael saith unto him, Whence knowest thou me? Jesus answered and said unto him, Before Philip called thee, when thou wast under the fig tree, I saw thee. Nathanael answered him, Rabbi, thou art the Son of God; thou art King of Israel. Jesus answered and said unto him, Because I said unto thee, I saw thee beneath the fig tree, believest thou? thou shalt see greater things than these. And he saith unto him, Verily, verily, I say unto you, Ye shall see the heaven opened, and the angels of God ascending and descending upon the Son of man" (John 1:47-51).

It was the custom of pious Jews to pray and meditate under a fig tree, and there Jesus had seen Nathanael before he came into His presence:

This would indicate that images of people and things are projected into the imaging chamber of the mind and that by giving them attention one can understand their relation to outer things. Mind readers, clairvoyants, and dreamers have developed this capacity in varying degree. Consciousness is what is concerned with soul unfoldment both primarily, and secondarily and all the way! Forms are always manifestations of ideas. Whoever understands this can interpret the symbols shown him in dreams and visions, but lack of understanding of this law makes one psychic without discernment.

With this spiritual faculty it is possible for man to penetrate into the "fourth dimension" or what is usually called the "kingdom of the heavens" and to discern the trend of the spiritual forces. The angels of God are spiritual forces active in the Sons of God, the spiritually quickened.

The open, receptive, and believing mind can see the things that take place in the Christ Mind, thus transcending the capacity of the unillumined natural man (MJ 22, 23).

Thus, five of the men who were eventually to become Jesus' apostles—Andrew, John, Peter, Philip, and Nathanael—became acquainted with Him and believed in Him at this time. Apparently, they did not leave their occupations and follow Him, as there is a record of Jesus' calling them later. However, they accompanied Him to Cana of Galilee where all attended a wedding feast. It was at this feast that Jesus performed His first miracle, the changing of water into wine.

A wedding was an event of great importance in Oriental countries and was lavishly celebrated. In wealthy families the festivities often lasted as long as seven days, and even among the poorer classes, one or two days were set aside for celebration. During this particular feast the wine supply was exhausted. As profuse hospitality was a point of honor among the Jews, this was a very embarrassing situation, almost a disgrace. Mary, the mother of Jesus, was among the guests, and she called her son's attention to the deficiency. "They have no wine," she said. "And Jesus saith unto her, Woman, what have I to do with thee? mine hour is not yet come" (John 2:4).

Jesus' seeming rebuke to His mother was not a show of disrespect, as "woman" was a common form of address in those days. His refusal means that when one is functioning in spiritual consciousness, as Jesus was, he is not moved to action until he is directed by the indwelling Christ. There is a divine fulfillment for every need, but Spirit cannot be coerced. "Mine hour is not yet come," Jesus said, inferring that He was not prompted to act even though He recognized the lack. Mary willingly acquiesced by saying to the servants, "Whatsoever he saith unto you, do it" (John 2:5), and Jesus, who was freed from any interference from the outer, took command of the situation:

Now there were six waterpots of stone set there after the Jews' manner of purifying, containing two or three firkins apiece. Jesus saith unto them, Fill the waterpots with water. And they filled them up to the brim. And he saith unto them, Draw out now, and bear unto the ruler of the feast. And they bare it. And when the ruler of the feast tasted the water now become wine and knew not whence it was (but the servants that had drawn the water knew), the ruler of the feast called the bridegroom, and saith unto him, Every man setteth on first the good wine; and when *men* have drunk freely, *then* that which is worse: thou hast kept the good wine until now (John 2:6-10).

A marriage is symbolic of the union of the consciousness with the indwelling Christ. Before such a union can take place, the negative state of mind (water) must be transmuted into positive spiritual life (wine):

The water pots filled to the brim with water by the servants represent the extent to which nature is prepared to fulfill the transformation from negative life to spiritual life through the power of the word of the Master, Jesus (MJ 25).

The miracle of changing the negative elements in consciousness into spiritual forces is performed in us when, by prayer, we unify our minds with Christ. Then He is in control, and our unregenerate thoughts and feelings are raised to spiritual heights. Thus, the holy marriage of the soul with Christ is consummated in harmony and joy. As a result, our outer needs are always filled in time to meet the demands (the water was made wine at the right moment). Also, the blessing that comes from Christ is superior to that which the mortal can produce (the ruler of the feast declared the new wine to be the best offered the guests), and it is abundant (more than enough was supplied).

CHAPTER IV

Early Judean Ministry

(First Year)

T HE TIME was drawing near for the celebration of the Passover, and Jesus returned to Jerusalem. As He entered the Temple on the first day of the feast, a scene of great confusion met His eyes. The spacious outer court, called the Court of the Gentiles, was the only place in the Temple precincts where Gentile converts were permitted to worship. In this court were stalls where oxen, sheep, and doves were sold for sacrifice. In addition, there were tables where money-changers were plying their trade, exchanging foreign coins for Jewish money, as the latter alone was acceptable for the annual Temple tax. As the bargaining for animals and arguments over values went on, loud voices rang out, and the atmosphere that prevailed was certainly not one of reverence.

It is probable that Jesus had witnessed this scene on many occasions and had objected inwardly, but this time the incongruity of it prompted Him to take action. Making a scourge of small cords, He "cast all out of the temple, both the sheep and the oxen; and he poured out the changers' money, and overthrew their tables; and to them that sold doves he said, Take these things hence; make not my Father's house a house of merchandise" (John 2:15, 16).

The Temple represents the body, the house of

Spirit. The body should be maintained as a fit place of worship, and its sanctity should be recognized. Often, however, our mental and emotional states are far from devout, and our bodies become infested with undesirable conditions that are evidence of greedy, material thoughts:

When we throw the light of Spirit into the subconscious courts of the body temple, we find queer and often startling conditions there. One would hardly expect to see butcher stalls and money-changers in a temple built for the worship of God, yet similar conditions exist in all of us.

So the body temple must be cleansed; it is the house of God ("for we are a temple of the living God"), and it should be put in order. The first step in this cleansing process is to recognize its need. The next step is the "scourge of small cords" (A.V.); to formulate the word or statement of denial. When we deny in general terms we cleanse the consciousness, but secret sins may yet lurk in the inner parts. The words that most easily reach these hidden errors are not great ones, such as "I am one with Almightiness; my environment is God" but small, definite statements that cut like whipcords into the sensuous, fleshly mentality (MJ 28, 29).

Those in charge of the Temple were incensed at what they considered Jesus' temerity in cleansing the court, and asked Him by what right He did this thing. His reply probably seemed rather irrelevant to them, for He said, "Destroy this temple, and in three days I will raise it up" (John 2:19). Because forty-six years had been required to build the Temple, Jesus' answer, then, was difficult for the Temple leaders to understand. "What could he mean"? they inquired. "But he spake of the temple of his body" (John 2:21). This was Jesus' first prediction that His body was to be resurrected.

Man's ability to preserve his body from destruction is the proof that he has mastered his mind. So long as our body shows signs of decay it is evident that we have not cast out of the inner realms the "thought butchers" that for a sacrifice kill doves, sheep, oxen, and goats. The allusion here is to the destructive thoughts lying deep in the consciousness at the very issue of life (MJ 32).

The three days that Jesus specified symbolize man's threefold nature—spirit, soul, and body. When one functions in spiritual consciousness, he has control over soul and body, and knows that the body can be resurrected ("in three days I will raise it up").

During His stay in Jerusalem, Jesus wrought miracles, and "many believed on his name" (John 2:23).

The Pharisees were the largest and most influential of the Jewish sects, and their ideal was to live in full accord with the will of God as it is revealed in both the written and the oral law. (The written law was the Mosaic law contained in the Old Testament; the oral law consisted of a great many explanations and interpretations of the written law that had been made by famous scribes and rabbis.)

Characteristic of the Pharisees was their religious zeal. Insisting on a strict observance of all cere-

monial requirements, they were considered very pious
by the masses of the people and exerted much influence over them. The great fault of the Pharisees
lay in the fact that they placed so much stress on
the outer forms of worship that they lost sight of
the inner spirit of it. By the beginning of the Christian era the Pharisees had, as a class, become narrow,
dogmatic, self-righteous, and conceited. Charles Fillmore states:

> In individual consciousness Pharisees represent thoughts
> that arise out of the subconsciousness, binding man to ex-
> ternal forms of religion without giving him understanding
> of their real meaning (MD 521).
>
> It is the Pharisee in us that causes us to love the
> forms and ceremonies of religion. It is the Pharisee in us
> that refuses to go deep into the consciousness and cleanse
> the inner man. It is the Pharisee in us that is ambitious for
> temporal honors and loves to be saluted with high-sounding
> titles. It is the pharisaical thought that exalts and sus-
> tains personality.
>
> We can overcome the Pharisee in ourselves by receiv-
> ing continuously new inspiration from the original fount
> of being within us, and by refusing to be bound by old,
> effete, religious thoughts (MD 522).

During His stay in Jerusalem, Jesus was visited
by Nicodemus, a leading Pharisee, and "a ruler of
the Jews" (John 3:1). This last phrase indicates
that Nicodemus was a member of the Jewish supreme court, called the Sanhedrin *(see Chap. X).*
Nicodemus came to see Jesus "by night," indicating
that he wished his visit to be in secret. Spiritually,
the night visit signifies that Nicodemus had intel-

.lectual but not spiritual understanding. Yet, in Nicodemus there was a perception of higher things than he had heretofore known, and he proved his willingness to learn by seeking out Jesus. Even though we may have been reared with dogmatic concepts of religion, spiritual light will be shown us if we seek for it.

Revealing his instinctive regard for Jesus, Nicodemus addressed Him as Rabbi, and said, "We know that thou art a teacher come from God; for no one can do these signs that thou doest, except God be with him" (John 3:2). Before he had a chance to say more, Jesus answered the question that was in His visitor's mind:

> Verily, verily, I say unto thee, Except one be born anew, he cannot see the kingdom of God. Nicodemus saith unto him, How can a man be born when he is old? . . . Jesus answered, Verily, verily, I say unto thee, Except one be born of water and the Spirit, he cannot enter into the kingdom of God. That which is born of the flesh is flesh; and that which is born of the Spirit is spirit. Marvel not that I said unto thee, Ye must be born anew. The wind bloweth where it will, and thou hearest the voice thereof, but knowest not whence it cometh, and whither it goeth: so is every one that is born of the Spirit (John 3:3-8).

Our innate desire is to progress spiritually; we want to "see the kingdom of God." But this is not possible until we are "born anew." We are born of the flesh, that is, we are living in a world where the sense or mortal consciousness governs, and in the main, our desires and interests have to do with the

satisfaction of the sense nature or with the seemingly
required routines of life. When we wish to be born
of Spirit, we must be willing and eager to come into
a higher state of consciousness. Jesus defined the
new birth as being "born of water and the Spirit."
Water cleanses and purifies. Water baptism signifies
repentance or a turning from the sense nature, a
denial of destructive thoughts and emotions. "To be
'born of the Spirit' is to come into the consciousness
of divine law and to lift the whole man into a
new life of harmony and order by affirmative prayer"
(MD 483).

Spirit is not a force that we have anything to do
with in the sense of creating it. Like the wind, it
"bloweth where it will," and we are aware of it. He
that is born of Spirit does not fully comprehend how
the change came about or when but he knows full
well that he is a different person. "The new birth
is simply the realization by man of his spiritual
identity, with the fullness of power and glory that
follows" (MJ 37, 38).

Nicodemus did not understand this and asked,
"How can these things be?" Before answering, Jesus
asked Nicodemus how it was that he, being a teacher
of Israel, could be ignorant of spiritual things. But
we know that many persons who make a study of
religious teachings are unaware of the action of
Spirit. Continuing His teaching, Jesus said, "No one
hath ascended into heaven, but he that descended out
of heaven, *even* the Son of man, who is in heaven"
(John 3:13).

There is but one real man, the ideal or spiritual man that God created. Jesus was explaining to Nicodemus the evolution of this spiritual man from his ideal to his manifest state. Man is fundamentally spiritual and so remains throughout his various manifestations. He comes out of heaven, manifests himself as a personality on the earth, and returns to heaven. . . . Faith in Spirit and the ultimate dominance of the good in man will finally restore him to the heaven from which he descended (MJ 37).

It is our privilege and responsibility to evolve from mortal to spiritual consciousness. "As Moses lifted up the serpent in the wilderness, even so must the Son of man be lifted up; that whosoever believeth may in him have eternal life" (John 3:14, 15). We are given the power to do this by our Creator: "For God so loved the world, that he gave his only begotten Son, that whosoever believeth on him should not perish, but have eternal life" (John 3:16).

The "only begotten Son" is the Christ within all men, the Spirit of God that is the very core of our being. God is love, and He gave of Himself to His offspring, man. We should acknowledge our divine sonship as well as believe in the divinity of Jesus. "This belief must then lead us to a desire and an effort to attain our inheritance, because then we know that there is no other thing in the universe worth striving for" (MJ 38).

Jesus explained that He, as God's Son, came into the world to save men, not to judge them, and:

He that believeth on him is not judged: he that believeth not hath been judged already, because he hath not believed on the name of the only begotten Son of God (John 3:18).

Salvation from sin, sickness, and sorrow begins when we have faith in Jesus as the Way-Shower and Saviour. Through the application of His teachings, we are saved from the dire effects of transgression. Jesus showed us the way of righteousness. Righteousness actually means the right or correct use of universal Principle. When we do not follow Him, we make the mistakes that belong to the human level of living and are "judged already"; we pay the penalty for deviating from the law of God, which rules supreme in the universe:

And this is the judgment, that the light is come into the world, and men loved the darkness rather than the light; for their works were evil. For every one that doeth ill hateth the light, and cometh not to the light, lest his works should be reproved. But he that doeth the truth cometh to the light, that his works may be made manifest, that they have been wrought in God (John 3:19-21).

Before a spiritual awakening we dwell in the ignorance or darkness of mortal concepts. As a result, our works are evil, and we "hate" the light. We begin to develop spiritually when we come "to the light." The way of righteousness is perceived, and we endeavor to follow it. We think differently; we act more worthily, and our works bear evidence that they "have been wrought in God."

For a time Jesus remained in Judea preaching

near the place where John the Baptist was conducting his ministry. After John was imprisoned by Herod Antipas, Jesus returned to Galilee. To make the trip He had to go through Samaria, a section of Palestine lying between Judea and Galilee.

The Judean Jews would have no dealings with the Samaritans, for they considered them of lower quality racially and religiously. The city of Samaria, from which the province took its name, was the capital of the old kingdom of Israel that had been conquered by Sargon II of Assyria in 722 B.C. Sargon deported thousands of the Hebrew inhabitants and imported various foreign tribes. During the passage of years the Hebrews who had been left in Israel intermarried with the foreigners, thus producing a mixed race. The religion of the Samaritans was similar to that of the Jews, for they accepted the Mosaic law and claimed Abraham as their ancestor. However, the Samaritans rejected the great Hebrew prophets and, both in ideals and practices, were inferior to the pure-blooded Jews. A Judean Jew felt himself vastly superior to a Samaritan and would not pass through the latter's territory if he could avoid it. Not so with Jesus. He felt that all men had equal standing in God's sight.

Samaria represents a mixed consciousness, partly worldly and partly religious, that results in a confused state of mind. Each of us in developing spiritually "must needs pass through Samaria" (John 4:4). And we may do so by allowing the Christ to instruct us.

When Jesus reached the Samaritan village of
Sychar, He sat down beside a well to rest while His
companions entered the village to buy food. A
woman came to the well to draw water, and Jesus
asked her to give Him a drink. It was not customary
for a Jew to ask anything of a Samaritan, and the
woman's surprise must have been apparent. Jesus
said:

If thou knewest the gift of God, and who it is that
saith to thee, Give me to drink; thou wouldest have asked
of him, and he would have given thee living water. The
woman saith unto him, Sir, thou hast nothing to draw
with, and the well is deep: whence then hast thou that
living water? Art thou greater than our Father Jacob,
who gave us the well, and drank thereof himself, and his
sons, and his cattle? Jesus answered and said unto her,
Every one that drinketh of this water shall thirst again:
but whosoever drinketh of the water that I shall give him
shall never thirst; but the water that I shall give him shall
become in him a well of water springing up unto eternal
life (John 4:10-14).

The Samaritan woman represents the soul that
has not yet been spiritually quickened:

But the soul must have Truth, and Christ recognizes
the soul as worthy; hence, this wonderful lesson of John
4:9-26 given to one auditor. The soul draws its life from
both the earthly side of existence (Jacob's well) and the
spiritual (the Jew), but is destined to draw from a higher
fount, omnipotent Spirit. Jesus asked the woman for a
drink, which indicates the universality of the spiritual
life, present in the Samaritan woman as well as in Jesus.

"The gift of God" to man is eternal life. The soul informed of this truth asks the Father for the manifestation of this life, and there gushes forth a never-failing stream. But where sense consciousness is dominant the soul is slow to see the realities of ideas, thoughts, and words; the sight is fixed on material ways and means: "Thou hast nothing to draw with . . . whence then hast thou that living water?" This is a fair setting forth of the status of the questioning ones of this day who ask the explanation of spiritual things on a material basis (MJ 47, 48).

In spite of the woman's doubt, Jesus offered to give her "living water" (spiritual inspiration) that would be an eternal blessing. The woman then said, "Sir, give me this water, that I thirst not, neither come all the way hither to draw" (John 4:15). Everyone longs for satisfaction but does not know how to attain it. Jesus called the woman's attention to the fact that He knew she was leading an immoral life and that this would deter her spiritual progress. She showed that she was willing to learn a higher way when she asked a question concerning worship:

Our fathers worshipped in this mountain; and ye say, that in Jerusalem is the place where men ought to worship. Jesus saith unto her, Woman, believe me, the hour cometh, when neither in this mountain, nor in Jerusalem, shall ye worship the Father. Ye worship that which ye know not: we worship that which we know; for salvation is from the Jews. But the hour cometh, and now is, when the true worshippers shall worship the Father in spirit and truth: for such doth the Father seek to be his worshippers. God is Spirit: and they that worship him must worship in spirit and truth (John 4:20-24).

Before we are attuned to Spirit we consider places and things as paramount, even in worshipping God. The Samaritan woman could not understand why the Jews believed that Jerusalem was the only proper place to worship. Spiritually interpreted, the Jews represent a higher concept of God; hence, Jesus' words, "Salvation is from the Jews." Yet the time comes when we need a more spiritual understanding of God and how to worship Him:

To worship God truly, we must know where He is and how to approach Him. If, as many teach, God lives in heaven, and heaven is located somewhere in the skies, we have a consciousness of separation from Him, and our approach to Him is uncertain.

But when we know the truth about God, that He is an omnipresent Spirit manifesting Himself to our mind, when we think of Him as one with us in Spirit and responding to our every thought, then we know Him as He is (MJ 46).

The woman avowed that she believed in the coming of the Messiah who "will declare unto us all things," and Jesus replied, "I that speak unto thee am *he*" (John 4:26). This was His first revelation to anyone of His true identity.

When Jesus' companions returned from the village they were astonished to find Him speaking to a woman, and especially a Samaritan. True, she had not understood the spiritual import of His words; nevertheless, she was impressed by them and particularly impressed by His knowledge of her personal life. She hastened to the village and reported

her unusual experience: "Can this be the Christ?"
she queried. Many of the villagers then started out
to find Jesus.

In the meantime, Jesus' companions urged Him
to eat the food they had brought:

> But he said unto them, I have meat to eat that ye
> know not. . . . My meat is to do the will of him that
> sent me, and to accomplish his work. Say not ye, There
> are yet four months, and *then* cometh the harvest? behold,
> I say unto you, Lift up your eyes, and look on the fields,
> that they are white already unto harvest. He that reapeth
> receiveth wages, and gathereth fruit unto life eternal; that
> he that soweth and he that reapeth may rejoice together.
> For herein is the saying true, One soweth and another
> reapeth. I sent you to reap that whereon ye have not
> labored; others have labored, and ye are entered into their
> labor (John 4:32-38).

Spiritual man (Jesus) draws on the substance of
divine ideas that nourish and sustain the consciousness. Jesus' ideal and mission was to do the Father's
will, and in speaking God's word to the woman of
Samaria, He was fulfilling His mission. Hence, He
felt a sense of satisfaction and completeness. Man
lives not by bread alone, but "by every word that
proceedeth out of the mouth of God" (Matt. 4:4).
The divine word is revealed to us when we love
God and share His freeing Truth with others. Those
who are still expressing in human consciousness
(Jesus' companions) are not aware of this inner
nourishment. They think that man is dependent on
the outer (planting and harvesting) for food. To

one of higher vision, the fields are "white already unto harvest," meaning that the pure substance of Spirit, which is the source of both inner and outer sustenance, is now at hand and can be appropriated by all. The one who knows God and does His will "reapeth" and gathers fruit "unto life eternal"; that is, he feels the quickening of Spirit and experiences the joy of expressing his divine attributes. Jesus had made this spiritual attainment ("one soweth"), and He was willing to share His understanding with His companions ("another reapeth"), so that both He and they might "rejoice together."

Jesus was ever ready to give the Truth to all alike, be they publicans or sinners, Jews or Samaritans, proving that salvation is for anyone who will accept Christ and have faith in the spiritual kingdom. As Jesus finished speaking, the people of Sychar approached and "besought him to abide with them; and he abode there two days. And many more believed because of his word" (John 4:40, 41).

CHAPTER V

Great Galilean Ministry

(Second Year)

G ALILEE, the little country made famous through Jesus of Nazareth, consists for the most part of an elevated plateau, dropping on the east to the lovely harp-shaped Sea of Galilee (also called Gennesaret and Chinnereth, but now known as the Lake of Tiberias). The Jordan River flows into the Sea of Galilee from the north and from it toward the Dead Sea in Judea. In Jesus' time Galilee was a fertile land yielding abundant crops. The sea teemed with fish, and many Galileans were fishermen. Large towns and villages dotted the province, the three chief cities being Capernaum, Bethsaida, and Chorazin. The main highways from Egypt to Syria and from Phoenicia to Persia passed through Galilee, making it a center of traffic.

It was in this setting that Jesus began the second year of His ministry, sometimes referred to as the Galilean ministry, and also as the Year of Popularity. His activity was now incessant, His service was largely to the multitudes, and before the year ended Jesus' fame was ringing throughout the length and breadth of Palestine. When Jesus arrived in His home territory, "the Galilaeans received him, having seen all the things that he did in Jerusalem at the feast."

Jesus went first to Cana, where he had previously performed the miracle of turning the water to wine at a wedding party. It was here that a nobleman besought Jesus to heal his son, who was at the point of death. The nobleman felt that there was an immediate need of action and that it would be necessary for Jesus to accompany him to his son's bedside. But Jesus, well aware that God's power is omnipresent, told the nobleman, "Go thy way; thy son liveth," (John 4:50). Apparently the nobleman was impressed, for he hastened home, where he was met by servants bearing the glad news that his son had been healed, and at the very hour when Jesus had spoken the word. It is easy to imagine the nobleman's joy when he heard the good news, and from that time on, he and his household believed in the teachings of Jesus.

In the incident of the nobleman's son we have the first detailed account of an individual healing that Jesus performed. Besides a number of statements to the effect that He healed many persons, evidently in groups where He was teaching, more than twenty instances of individual healing are given in the Gospels. In most instances Jesus was in the presence of the sufferer, but there are several accounts of healings that were accomplished from a distance, such as the one related above.

The secret of spiritual healing is the recognition and acknowledgment of wholeness in the person who is expressing a physical limitation, and much effective healing is being done today through earnest prayer. It is not necessary for the sick person to be in the presence of the one or ones who are praying.

In the majority of the individual accounts of healings, Jesus merely spoke the word, such as, "Be thou made clean" (Matt. 8:3). In several instances, however, He performed an act, as when He "made clay of the spittle," anointed the eyes of the man born blind, and told him to wash in the pool of Siloam (John 9:1-7). Jesus' course in doing something for the afflicted person, and telling him to do something for himself, seems to have been for the purpose of strengthening the man's faith. It is occasionally effective in our healing work today to combine prayer and action. Healing can only result when faith enters in, but often the act tends to increase faith.

Among Jesus' healings there is at least one where a partial healing preceded a complete cure (Mark 8:22-25). In this case, Jesus put His hands on the eyes of the blind man, and the man reported that he saw men "as trees, walking." Jesus again placed His hands on the man's eyes, and his sight was wholly restored. This should encourage us. Often our own healings and those for whom we pray are gradual, but they can be instantaneous, as they generally were when Jesus spoke the word of wholeness. In the event our faith is not sufficient to accept a complete restoration immediately, we should understand that an improvement in the condition is evidence of the activity of Spirit. Our part is to continue to pray until the full healing is accomplished. Charles Fillmore says:

Ability to pick up the life current and through it perpetually to vitalize the body is based on the right relation of ideas, thoughts, and words. These mental impulses start currents of energy that form and also stimulate molecules and cells already formed, producing life, strength, and animation where inertia and impotence was the dominant appearance. This was and is the healing method of Jesus" (JC 4).

The healings that Jesus performed, covering as they did every sort of physical and mental deficiency, are considered miracles. To them should be added the three occasions on which He raised persons from the dead: the son of the widow of Nain (Luke 7:11-17), the daughter of Jairus (Matt. 9:18-26), and Lazarus (John 11:1-46). In addition, He performed other miracles of a general nature, such as healing the lunatic child (Matt. 17:14), multiplying the loaves and fishes to feed five thousand (Matt. 14:13-23), and walking on the water (Matt. 14:24-36).

What is a miracle? One dictionary defines a miracle as, "an event or effect in the physical world deviating from the known laws of nature, or transcending our knowledge of these laws." According to this definition, Jesus did perform miracles. Many Christians contend that miraculous power was given only to Jesus and His immediate followers. Metaphysically, a miracle is explained as being the outcome of man's obedience to divine law. Jesus gave His whole attention to God and thus established a union with the creative life within Him. Being master of Himself, He had dominion over all conditions and asserted the authority that was given to man in the beginning. He said, however, "He that believeth on me"; that is, believes in the reality of spiritual man, "the works that I do shall he do also and greater *works* than these shall he do" (John 14:12). Jesus' real mission was to teach us to follow Him by lifting our consciousness from the sense level to a spiritual level. Every person is made in the image and likeness of God. When he realizes this, and lives in harmony with the indwelling Christ, he is able to use his power to bring about conditions that may seem miraculous to one who is functioning in human consciousness.

Jesus did not perform His great works (miracles) in an effort to draw attention to Himself and thus gain a following; neither were they done to satisfy the curiosity of the people. They were done to glorify God and to bring about wholeness. The Pharisees frequently demanded a sign that He (Jesus) was sent of God, and Jesus consistently refused, saying, "An evil and adulterous generation seeketh after a sign; and there shall no sign be given unto it, but the sign of Jonah" (Matt. 16:4). He demanded faith from persons whom He healed, and His works were done to help mankind. He often "charged them that they should tell no man" (Mark 7:36). Such deeds were impossible to hide even in individual cases. Many of the miracles were performed in the presence of groups. Therefore, with each deed of mercy His fame increased.

From Cana, where He had healed the noble-

man's son, Jesus went to His home town of Nazareth. On the Sabbath He attended the local synagogue. Every city or town of any size had one or
more synagogues where services were held regularly.
The services were under the jurisdiction of elders,
and the chief officer was known as the Ruler of the
Synagogue. In contrast to the elaborate ceremonies in
the Temple at Jerusalem, which only priests could
conduct, the service in a synagogue was simple, and
frequently a layman was invited to participate. On
this occasion Jesus was asked to take part, and He
was handed the book of the prophet Isaiah from
which to read. He selected these significant verses:

The Spirit of the Lord is upon me,
Because he anointed me to preach good tidings to the poor:
He hath sent me to proclaim release to the captives,
And recovering of sight to the blind,
To set at liberty them that are bruised,
To proclaim the acceptable year of the Lord
                                        (Luke 4:18, 19).

Handing the book back to the clerk, Jesus sat
down to deliver His sermon, a customary practice
among the Jews. "And he began to say unto them,
To-day hath this scripture been fulfilled in your
ears" (Luke 4:21). This was equivalent to saying
that He was the Messiah prophesied by Isaiah and
that He was to fulfill the works of the Anointed of
God. This announcement so amazed His hearers that
they began to murmur, "Is not this Joseph's son?"
(Luke 4:22). They could not conceive of one of

their own neighbors as being the promised Messiah. Jesus' defense of His position filled them with wrath. They took hold of Him and led Him to the brow of a hill from which they intended to cast Him down. "But he passing through the midst of them went his way" (Luke 4:30). This eluding of the angry crowd was a most unusual occurrence and is thought-provoking. Jesus did not have to fight His way out of this difficult situation. Apparently, it was handled calmly and easily. He trusted His Father to care for Him in His time of need. We can do likewise and we do not have to know just how we shall be protected.

Perhaps it was this rejection at Nazareth that led Jesus to select Capernaum as the headquarters for His Galilean ministry. As He was walking by the Sea of Galilee, He called four men to be His apostles —Peter, Andrew, James, and John, the last two being the sons of Zebedee. Jesus' invitation was, "Come ye after me, and I will make you fishers of men" (Matt. 4:19). Three of these men, Andrew, Peter, and John, were with Jesus at least part of the time in His early Judean ministry; yet it was at the time of this calling that they left their homes and occupations and "followed him." The Gospels give an account of Jesus' calling only one other apostle. This was Matthew, a publican and a Jew, who collected taxes for the Roman government. Those who served in the capacity of publican were despised by the Jews, for the position lent itself to corruption, oppression, and abuse. But Matthew, at the call of

Jesus, "forsook all, and rose up and followed him"
(Luke 5:28).

Jesus performed many healings in Capernaum
and the surrounding territory, and these, together
with His teachings, attracted the attention of the
scribes and Pharisees. The scribes, most of whom
were Pharisees, were Jewish scholars and profes-
sional interpreters of the law, sometimes referred
to as lawyers or doctors of the law. The scribes
copied the Hebrew Scriptures into Aramaic, the
language generally spoken in Palestine. In addition,
they made new regulations, called in the Gospels
"the traditions of the elders" (Matt. 15:2).

At the start of Jesus' ministry in Galilee, the
scribes and Pharisees seemed to be genuinely interested in what He said and did. "And they were astonished at his teaching: for he taught them as having authority, and not as the scribes" (Mark 1:22).
It was the custom of the scribes to read the law and
to quote profusely from the writings of learned rabbis. Here was a man speaking on His own authority.
They listened and marveled when He healed a
demoniac (Mark 1:21-28) and a leper (Mark 1:40-
45). But Jesus soon antagonized them by healing on
the Sabbath. To them this constituted a violation of
their law, for a rigid observance of Sabbath rules
and regulations was sacred to them. Jesus maintained, "It is lawful to do good on the sabbath day"
(Matt. 12:12). When the Pharisees objected to
Jesus' disciples plucking corn as they went through
the grainfields on the Sabbath, He declared, "The

sabbath was made for man, and not man for the sabbath" (Mark 2:27). They considered it sacrilegious
when He said to a paralytic whom He healed, "Thy
sins are forgiven" (Matt. 9:2). They believed that
only God can forgive sins. Jesus' reply was, "The
Son of man hath authority on earth to forgive sins"
(Matt. 9:6).

Forgiveness really means the giving up of something.
When you forgive yourself, you cease doing the thing that
you ought not to do. Jesus was correct in assuming that
man has power to forgive sin. Sin is a falling short of the
divine law, and repentance and forgiveness are the only
means that man has of getting out of sin and its effect
and coming into harmony with the law. . . . Some mental
attitude, some train of mental energy, must be transformed.
We forgive sin in ourselves every time we resolve to think
and act according to the divine law (JC 58, 59).

In still other ways, Jesus' actions antagonized the
Jewish leaders. To them it was inconceivable that a
religious teacher would associate with publicans and
sinners. Yet Jesus had feasted with them at a dinner
given in His honor by Matthew, the publican, and
had defended His position by saying, "They that are
whole have no need of a physician, but they that are
sick. . . . I came not to call the righteous, but sinners" (Matt. 9:12, 13). He well knew that His mission was to the outcasts as well as other needy persons.

The Pharisees were also displeased that neither
Jesus nor His disciples fulfilled the requirements of
the oral law as it applied to fasting. Even the dis-

ciples of John the Baptist, who was himself somewhat revolutionary in his preaching, complied with
this provision. Jesus reminded those who asked for
an explanation that it was not wise to sew a new
piece of cloth on an old garment nor put new wine
into old wineskins. This implied that the new teachings that He was giving could not fit into the pat-
terns of old beliefs to which the Pharisees had become bound (Matt. 9:16-17). Metaphysically, the
Pharisees represent a phase of consciousness that ad-
heres to the outer observance of religion, and Jesus
represents the higher consciousness that knows itself
to be one with Spirit.

During the second year of His ministry Jesus
went to Jerusalem to attend a feast, possibly the
Passover. At the pool of Bethesda Jesus healed a
man who had been lame for thirty-eight years (John
5:1-47). On this occasion the Pharisees were doubly
offended, for Jesus not only healed on the Sabbath
but He called God His Father. To them, such action
was blasphemy. To this charge Jesus replied, "Verily,
verily, I say unto you, The Son can do nothing of
himself, but what he seeth the Father doing . . . For
the Father loveth the Son, and showeth him all
things that himself doeth . . . For as the Father
raiseth the dead and giveth them life, even so the
Son also giveth life to whom he will" (John 5:19-
21). Jesus understood that the Son (conscious self)
can do nothing unless unified with the Father (super-
consciousness or Christ self). However, when this
union has been made, one is aware of the power of

the indwelling Christ and can speak the healing word.

The Pharisees, symbolizing the attitude of mind that loves the outer observance of religion, could not heal. They did not understand that they, too, had access to the Spirit of truth within them and that they could and should claim oneness with it. Jesus knew He was one with the Father, and He spoke in that consciousness. To those who were still on a lower level of thought, such a realization as Jesus had was a mystery of which they were skeptical, critical, and antagonistic. In His contests with the Pharisees Jesus was always able to silence them temporarily with His logical replies, but a smoldering anger and resentment stirred within them, which was to burst into violent hostility later on.

After Jesus returned to Galilee He was followed by great crowds that pressed around Him. Word of His marvelous healings had traveled like wildfire through Palestine and even to Phœnicia. Many who were ill came to Him, along with the throngs that were attracted by His teaching. "And he spake to his disciples, that a little boat should wait on him because of the crowd, lest they should throng him" (Mark 3:9). The little boat was to become His favorite pulpit, and from it He taught and healed the multitude that gathered on the shore of the sea.

Finally, from the many who followed Him, Jesus selected twelve men to be His apostles. He had previously accepted seven of them (Andrew, Peter, James and John [sons of Zebedee], Philip, Barthol-

omew, and Matthew. Judas Iscariot was the only
apostle who was a Judean; all the others were Galileans. Jesus had prayed all night before making this
important decision. Luke tells us:

> And when it was day, he called his disciples; and he
> chose from them twelve, whom also he named apostles:
> Simon, whom he also named Peter, and Andrew his brother,
> and James and John, and Philip and Bartholomew, and
> Matthew and Thomas, and James *the son* of Alphaeus, and
> Simon who was called the Zealot, and Judas *the son* of
> James, and Judas Iscariot, who became a traitor (Luke
> 6:13-16).

Metaphysically, the apostles represent the twelve
spiritual qualities or powers within man. These
powers have their origin in the superconscious or
spiritual phase of mind, but they function through
the subconscious mind. Charles Fillmore states:

> When Jesus Christ had attained a certain soul develop-
> ment, he called His twelve disciples to Him. This means
> that when man is developing out of mere personal con-
> sciousness into spiritual consciousness, he begins to train
> deeper and larger powers . . . Where before his powers
> have worked in the personal, now they begin to expand
> and work in the universal (TM 15).

It is our privilege to call these great faculties
(apostles) from the mortal, where they have been
expressing, to the spiritual where their work becomes much more effectual, and each is of vital importance and necessary to the unfoldment of the
Christ self. Jesus chose the Twelve just before He

gave the Sermon on the Mount. Before we can fully comprehend the vital and lofty meaning of the Sermon, these twelve spiritual powers within us must be quickened.

The apostle Peter represents faith. "We begin our religious experience, our unity with Divine Mind, by having faith in that Mind as omnipresent, all-wise, all-loving, and all-powerful Spirit" (TM 17). Faith is thus the essential foundation for the building of a spiritual consciousness. At first faith is wavering and changeable, as was Peter when he became frightened while walking on the water, and when, in fear, he denied knowing Jesus.

You must teach Peter to concentrate. Teach him to center on true words. It is through him that you feed your sheep, your other faculties. Keep him right at his task. He is inquisitive, impulsive, and dictatorial, when not firmly directed. When he questions your dominion and tries to dictate the movements of your other powers, put him in line with, "What is that to thee? follow thou me" (MD 518).

If we continue to affirm our faith in God, a steadfast faith becomes established in us and is the rock upon which our church (spiritual consciousness) is built.

The apostle Andrew represents strength. In man strength is thought of primarily as physical stamina, to which man adds strength of purpose and moral character as he develops. When it is raised to a spiritual level strength enables a person to overcome

human might. David was able to slay Goliath because he had the strength of Spirit.

Be steadfast, strong, and steady in thought, and you
will establish strength in soul and in body. Never let the
thought of weakness enter your consciousness, but always
ignore the suggestion and affirm yourself to be a tower of
strength, within and without (TM 38).

The apostle James, the son of Zebedee, represents wisdom and judgment. James is the faculty in
us by which we weigh a matter and come to a con-
clusion. When judgment is divorced from wisdom its
conclusions are faulty and lead to condemnation
and criticism. Through the faithful affirmation of
wisdom and good judgment, the spiritual aspect of
this power comes into activity.

When we awaken to the reality of our being, the light
begins to break upon us from within and we know the
truth; this is the quickening of our James or judgment
faculty. When this quickening occurs, we find ourselves
discriminating between the good and the evil. We no
longer accept the race standards or the teachings of the
worldly wise, but we "judge righteous judgment"; we
know with an inner intuition, and we judge men and
events from a new viewpoint (TM 44).

The apostle John represents love. John is also
the son of Zebedee and, therefore, the brother of
James. Wisdom and love are closely related and
should function in unison. Wisdom may be harsh
without love, and love may be foolish without wisdom. When spiritual love is quickened it becomes a

healing, harmonizing force in the life of an individual. Jesus summed up the Ten Commandments in two great ones that are based on love: "Thou shalt love the Lord thy God with all thy heart, and with all thy soul, and with all thy mind, and with all thy strength. The second is this, Thou shalt love thy neighbor as thyself" (Mark 12:30, 31). We recognize God as law through the wisdom or judgment faculty, James; we fulfill the law through the love faculty, John.

Philip represents power. Power is the ability to do, to perform, and to accomplish. In unredeemed man power is expressed in selfish ways to gain what man wishes to have in the material world. The power God has given us is the dominion and mastery over ourselves. "He that ruleth his spirit" is more powerful "than he that taketh a city" (Prov. 16:32).

In the process of regeneration the consciousness of power ebbs and flows, because the old and the new tides of thought act and react in the conscious and subconscious realms of mind. However, when a disciple realizes his unity with Omnipotence he is but little disturbed by the changes that go on in his mind and his body. He knows that his spiritual dominion is established, and this firm conviction expresses itself in firm words. . . . Jesus said, "Heaven and earth shall pass away, but my words shall not pass away." Here is evidence of spiritual power united with the idea of eternity (MD 525).

The risen Jesus said to His apostles, "Ye shall receive power, when the Holy Spirit is come upon you" (Acts 1:8). When the spiritual consciousness is quickened, there is an inflow of power from on high (the Christ center of our being).

Bartholomew, called Nathanael in the Gospel of John, represents imagination. All visible forms have their origin in the imagination, and it is through the activity of this faculty that the formless takes form, thus molding our bodies and the conditions of our lives. The Lord instructed Moses to make all things "after their pattern, which hath been showed thee in the mount" (Exod. 25:40). The mount represents the spiritual consciousness; therefore, we are to make (image) in accord with our highest realizations. It is our right to call on Bartholomew when things look dark, and through the faculty of the spiritual imagination we see the silver lining of the cloud— health instead of sickness, opulence instead of lack, peace instead of inharmony.

Thomas represents understanding. In the human consciousness understanding is related to intellect but it is attuned to wisdom in spiritual consciousness. We should have an intuitive knowledge that is based on spiritual perception, and not on reason.

When we discover in ourselves a flow of thought that seems to have evolved independently of the reasoning process, we are often puzzled about its origin and its safety as a guide. In its beginnings this seemingly strange source of knowledge is often turned aside as a daydream; again it seems a distant voice, an echo of something that we have heard and forgotten. One should give attention to this un-usual and usually faint whispering of Spirit in man. It is not of the intellect . . . It is the development, in man, of a greater capacity to know himself and to understand the purpose of creation. . . . It is accredited [in the Bible] as coming from the heart. The nature of the process is not explained; one who is in the devotional stage of unfoldment need not know all the complex movements of the mind in order to get the message of the Lord. It is enough to know that the understanding is opened in both head and heart when man gives himself wholly to the Lord (TM 90).

Matthew represents the will. The will is the executive power of the mind and is the focal point around which all our actions center. It is the power to act decisively. Man is a free agent who possesses and uses this faculty.

The will always enters into man's decisions. The will makes the final choice to give up all and follow Jesus. . . . The will has been given over to the thought of accumulation by imposition on external resources. In the regeneration the will is converted, and is taught by prayer and meditation how to stabilize the universal substance . . . When the individual will has become a disciple of the Christ, spiritual I AM, the schooling of the man begins (MD 434).

The highest office of the will is to unify itself with divine will. This is exemplified in Jesus' prayer, "Not my will, but thine, be done" (Luke 22:42).

James, the son of Alphæus, represents law and order. Order is termed "heaven's first law," and Paul cautions, "Let all things be done decently and in order" (I Cor. 14:40).

Man can never exercise dominion until he knows who and what he is and, knowing, brings forth that knowledge

into the external by exercising it in divine order, which
is mind, idea, and manifestation (TM 113).

Jesus outlined the orderly procedure for our spiritual progress when He said, "First the blade, then
the ear, then the full grain in the ear" (Mark 4:28).
The blade represents the period when Truth is being
implanted in the mind; the ear signifies the growth
and development of spiritual ideas; and the full
grain in the ear is the manifestation or bringing forth
of these ideas. In our unfoldment we are prone to
disregard this orderly sequence and attempt to jump
from blade to full grain. This is as impossible as trying to leap from infancy to adulthood. In all ways
growth should be orderly if it is to follow the harmonious laws of the universe. Both as regards our
inner and outer lives we need to understand God's
law and co-operate with it in an orderly manner.

Simon the Zealot represents zeal.

Zeal is the mighty force that incites the winds, the
tides, the storms; it urges the planet on its course, and
spurs the ant to greater exertion. To be without zeal is to
be without the zest of living. Zeal and enthusiasm incite
to glorious achievement in every aim and ideal that the
mind conceives. Zeal is the impulse to go forward, the urge
behind all things. Without zeal stagnation, inertia, death
would prevail throughout the universe. The man without
zeal is like an engine without steam or an electric motor
without a current. Energy is zeal in motion, and energy is
the forerunner of every effect (TM 130).

We should not repress zeal but, on the other
hand, care should be taken to keep zeal balanced

with wisdom. Paul says, "They have a zeal for God, but not according to knowledge" (Rom. 10:2).

One may even become so zealous for the spread of Truth as to bring on nervous prostration. "Take time to be holy." Turn a portion of your zeal to do God's will to the establishing of His kingdom within you. Do not put all your enthusiasm into teaching, preaching, healing, and helping others; help your own soul. Many enthusiastic spiritual workers have let their zeal to demonstrate Truth to others rob them of the power to demonstrate Truth for themselves. Do not let your zeal run away with your judgment (TM 132, 133).

Thaddæus, the son of James, called Judas in Luke's Gospel, represents renunciation. To renounce means to relinquish or eliminate. In the process of spiritual unfoldment we must renounce many false beliefs and destructive emotions.

It is just as necessary that one should learn to let go of thoughts, conditions, and substances in consciousness, body, and affairs, when they have served their purpose and one no longer needs them, as it is that one should lay hold of new ideas and new substances to meet one's daily requirements. Therefore, it is very necessary that the eliminative faculty be quickened in one, and a right balance between receiving and giving, laying hold and letting go, be established (MD 653).

When we love God we are willing to renounce the things in our consciousness and outer lives that do not belong to our spiritual natures.

Judas Iscariot represents life. In Judas we find the unredeemed life forces that, unless handled spir-

itually, betray the Christ or spiritual self. The Christ
life within us is pure and undefiled, but we, as individuals, can use this life energy any way we
choose. Since men have used their lives destructively
they have been deprived of their bodies. When we
expend this life force in the satisfaction of sense desires and pleasures we pervert it; devastation of mind
and body then results. Judas was the treasurer for
Jesus and His apostles. He held the moneybag, and
greed and covetousness ruled in him:

> The first step in our redeeming the Judas faculty is to
> assume a fearless attitude of mind, affirming our unity with
> the Spirit of purity. When we do this the Lord answers,
> "Thou hast said," and the redeeming, uplifting, transmut-
> ing forces are set into operation. When the Judas faculty
> reaches the spiritual standard of life it is known as Judah,
> whose office is praise and thanksgiving. Praise and thanks-
> giving call into activity greater expressions of spiritual
> substance and open larger avenues through which we may
> receive spiritual life. Praise radiates and gives glory to the
> latent powers of man (MD 375).

When we are tempted to succumb to sense desires of an unworthy nature, it means that Judas is
in control. In giving our attention to Christ as Jesus
did, the greedy, selfish sense desires are eliminated
(Judas is repentant and kills himself), thus giving
the higher consciousness full reign to assert itself.
To fill the place in their group that was left vacant
by Judas, the apostles chose Matthias, who represents the lifting up of the life faculty "that it may
aid the individual in laying hold of his higher spir-

itual attainments . . . through the power of his in-dwelling Christ" (MD 434).

Thus, when man has brought his higher self into action, he will see clearly the relation of spirit, soul, and body. Jesus taught that the goal of man is eternal life. Only those who have strengthened their faculties can appreciate the wonderful undeveloped possibilities in man; the spiritually minded man beholds them as all-potential (TM 173).

CHAPTER VI

The New Law

(Second Year)

SOON AFTER the selection of the Twelve Apostles, Jesus delivered the immortal lessons that comprise the Sermon on the Mount. Even as the law that Moses received on Mount Sinai is the heart of Judaism, the Sermon on the Mount is the heart of Christianity. The Sermon is the new law; it is not meant to abrogate the revered Mosaic law but it is to teach us how this law may be fulfilled spiritually. The first law given to Moses, and which came from the heights of Sinai in the wilderness, was accompanied by thunders and lightnings. The new law was enunciated from the summit of a grassy hill in Galilee, probably from an elevation known as the Horns of Hattin, as its two peaks resemble an Oriental saddle. Here a crowd gathered to see and hear the Master, whose words were spoken in quietness and in love. The "Thou shalt not" of the Ten Commandments is replaced by the words "Blessed are ye" in the Sermon on the Mount. The Decalogue's stern delineation of right and wrong is mitigated in the Sermon to a compassionate appeal for righteous thinking and feeling. Moses stated the law; Jesus explained the way to obey it. We read in Matt. 5:1-11:

And seeing the multitudes, he [Jesus] went up into the

mountain: and when he had sat down, his disciples came
unto him; and he opened his mouth and taught them,
saying,

> Blessed are the poor in spirit; for theirs is the
> kingdom of heaven.

This is the first of the eight great statements
called the Beatitudes. Each statement says that we
shall be blessed when we attain certain attitudes of
mind. The "poor in spirit" are persons who relinquish their human concepts that they may learn
from God. The intellect of man is marvelous indeed; yet, if we are to attain divine wisdom we
must be humble (poor in spirit) toward Him and
willing and eager to hear His words and follow
them. This is the only way that our mind can expand Godward. As our mind develops, we come into
the realization of the omnipresent good (the kingdom of heaven).

> Blessed are they that mourn: for they shall be
> comforted.

Trials and tribulations cause us to mourn. Yet
it is true that "Man's extremity is God's opportunity," and when woes beset us we turn to Him and
receive comfort.

> Blessed are the meek: for they shall inherit the
> earth.

Meekness, spiritually considered, is an attitude
of receptivity to the divine will. Jesus was meek

when He said, "Not as I will, but as thou wilt."
Meekness is a willingness to surrender to God and
a confidence that His way is the better way. When
the Christ expresses through us, we have power over
external conditions (the earth).

> Blessed are they that hunger and thirst after right-
> eousness: for they shall be filled.

Righteousness is the right or spiritual use of
mental, physical, and spiritual faculties, which are
manifested as right action. When our desire to express the Christ is more powerful than our desire for
personal gain or for personal power, we are hun-
gering and thirsting after righteousness. The promise
is that we shall be filled; that is, our desire shall be
satisfied by divine love and divine life.

> Blessed are the merciful: for they shall obtain
> mercy.

The merciful are persons who are kind in thought
and in deed. On occasion we may feel impelled to
help someone but we do it reluctantly. Such acts
fall short of true mercy because thought and deed
are at variance. We are only merciful when we realize that all men are brothers and that the good of
one is the good of all, and act accordingly. We always receive mercy in proportion to our being merciful.

> Blessed are the pure in heart: for they shall see
> God.

Pure means unmixed, chaste, and free from defilement. A person whose heart is pure directs his whole attention to God, to good. Purity is one-pointed vision, the "single" eye. Impurity, in a spiritual sense, implies double vision, seeing good and evil. When the consciousness is so purified that we perceive only one Presence and One Power, we are, in reality, seeing God.

> Blessed are the peacemakers: for they shall be
> called sons of God.

The peacemakers are persons who make peace outwardly because they have attained an inner peace. Since they are at peace with God they are also at peace with others, and they bring peace to all the conditions in which they are involved. We are sons of God, but our sonship is merely an inherent potentiality until we gain peace of mind and express it. Then we are His sons in actuality (called sons of God).

> Blessed are they that have been persecuted for
> righteousness' sake: for theirs is the kingdom of
> heaven. Blessed are ye when men shall reproach
> you, and persecute you, and say all manner of evil
> against you falsely, for my sake. Rejoice, and be
> exceeding glad: for great is your reward in heaven.

Persons who are persecuted for righteousness' sake are ones who have spiritual ideals and yet encounter within themselves states of consciousness that oppose their ideals. These adverse states of consciousness belong to the race thought, much of which is still in each of us. These states are tenacious and unyielding and resist or persecute the ideals that we are endeavoring to maintain. Not only is there an inner conflict; there may be an outer one also: "men shall reproach you, and persecute you." When people do not understand our spiritual convictions they are apt to misjudge and condemn us. This beatitude promises that we shall be blessed if we maintain our ideals in the face of inner and outer persecution. We should actually rejoice and be "exceeding glad," for our steadfastness will bring great spiritual advancement. This is our "reward in heaven," and heaven is the spiritual kingdom within all men.

From these basic statements that concern spiritual thought and feeling, Jesus proceeded with a more detailed account to show that the new law was to be put into operation through better understanding. He revealed man's true identity by saying, "Ye are the salt of the earth" (Matt. 5:13) and "Ye are the light of the world" (Matt. 5:14). But He warned that the salt can lose its savor, and the light is often put under a bushel. This means that when we do not recognize our spiritual natures we lack the ability to express the power that is rightfully ours. Rather:

Let your light shine before men; that they may see your good works, and glorify your Father who is in heaven (Matt. 5:16).

In the hands of the Jewish leaders of Jesus' day,

the Mosaic law had become a routine of exaggerated scruples and formalism from which Spirit had been banished. Jesus clearly stated His position with reference to the law: "Think not that I came to destroy the law or the prophets: I came not to destroy, but to fulfil" (Matt. 5:17). Nevertheless, our obedience to the law should "exceed *the righteousness* of the scribes and Pharisees" (Matt. 5:20); that is, it should be of the Spirit and not merely of the letter.

Jesus showed the difference between the manner in which the law was being obeyed and the requirements for its spiritual fulfillment. He enjoined forgiveness ("be reconciled to thy brother"), nonresistance ("resist not him that is evil"), morality in thought as well as in act ("every one that looketh on a woman to lust after her hath committed adultery with her already in his heart"), a willingness to give more than is asked ("whosoever shall compel thee to go one mile, go with him two"), and loving and praying for our enemies ("love your enemies, and pray for them that persecute you"). "Ye therefore shall be perfect, as your heavenly Father is perfect" (Matt. 5:24-48).

Alms should be given modestly, not with ostentation. We should not flaunt our piety before men, but display it for God only. "When thou prayest, enter into thine inner chamber, and having shut thy door, pray to thy Father who is in secret, and thy Father who seeth in secret shall recompense thee" (Matt. 6:6).

The inner chamber signifies the inmost recesses of our being. It is sometimes referred to as the upper room or chamber, and the Psalmist poetically calls this inner sanctuary the "secret place of the Most High." It is here that we become aware of our one-ness with God. As we enter the inner chamber by opening our consciousness to Him, our mind is closed to worldly considerations ("having shut thy door"). Frequently the mind is so filled with outer interests it is difficult to release them and think of God. If persistent, we learn the secret of spiritual concentration and abide in the secret place. The prayer that we then make is in obedience to the rules of prayer, and we may rest in the promise that "thy Father who seeth in secret shall recompense thee."

That His hearers might know how to pray aright Jesus gave a model for all true prayer, The Lord's Prayer. It is all-inclusive, encompassing the entire category of human needs. Regardless of what words we use in any prayer they touch the Lord's Prayer at some point. This mighty prayer, familiar as it is to every Christian, becomes a vital part of our prayer life when our understanding of it deepens:

"Our Father (the one life that all share) who art in heaven (the spiritual realm), Hallowed be thy name (holy is Thy nature).

"Thy kingdom come (the wholeness of Thy spirit be manifested).

"Thy will be done in earth, as it is heaven (Thy perfect will come into expression on the plane of manifestation, earth, as it is on the spiritual heights).

"Give us this day our daily bread (all that is necessary to sustain life spiritually, mentally, and physically).

"And forgive us our debts, as we also have forgiven our debtors (as we forgive others their trespasses against us, we are forgiven).

"And leave us not in temptation, but deliver us from evil. (This is perhaps the least understood portion of the prayer. God who is perfect good could never bring or lead or leave us in temptation, but it is undoubtedly true that we are tested. This portion of the prayer asks that we may be delivered from the seeming powers of evil).

"For thine is the kingdom, and the power, and the glory, for ever (is our recognition that God is the giver of all good, and we acknowledge His supremacy).

"Amen (so be it, is our acceptance in faith)."

True prayers accumulate "treasures in heaven," i.e. a rich consciousness filled with faith and peace, where "neither moth nor rust doth consume, and where thieves do not break through nor steal" (Matt. 6:20). Jesus pointed out that the "single" eye (seeing God only) brings wholeness to our life and frees us from the darkness or limitation that comes from seeing good and evil.

No man can serve two masters; for either he will hate the one, and love the other; or else he will hold to one, and despise the other. Ye cannot serve God and mammon (Matt. 6:24).

Cares and anxieties as regards the material necessities of life should not divert our attention. Our first desire should be to serve God. "Your heavenly Father knoweth that ye have need of all these things. But seek ye first his kingdom, and his righteousness; and all these things shall be added unto you" (Matt. 6:32, 33). Jesus reminds us that our heavenly Father is even more desirous of giving "good things to them that ask him" (Matt. 7:11) than is an earthly father. Therefore,

Ask, and it shall be given you: seek, and ye shall find; knock, and it shall be opened unto you: for every one that asketh receiveth; and he that seeketh findeth; and to him that knocketh it shall be opened (Matt. 7:7, 8).

The law of life gives perfect justice to all, and Jesus cautions us not to judge if we do not want to be judged. "For with what judgment ye judge, ye shall be judged: and with what measure ye mete, it shall be measured unto you" (Matt. 7:2). Why should we look for the faults of others when our own are close at hand and need correcting? "Thou hypocrite, cast out first the beam out of thine eye; and then shalt thou see clearly to cast out the mote out of thy brother's eye" (Matt. 7:5).

Jesus instructed His listeners to enter in "by the narrow gate." Narrow, indeed, is the gate and straight the way "that leadeth unto life" (the more abundant life of Spirit), but "few are they that find it." Many persons take the broad way that appears to be easier, but it "leadeth to destruction" (Matt.

7:13, 14). It is given to each of us to choose the way he will take.

Jesus cautioned us against "false prophets"; that is, He warned us of certain religious teachers. These persons promise much, but they have nothing to offer in the way of spiritual virtues. The corrupt tree can bring forth only evil fruit, but the good tree brings forth good fruit. If we do the "will of my Father" we produce good fruit, and "by their fruits ye shall know them."

Jesus ended the Sermon on the Mount by drawing a contrast between persons who hear His sayings and disregard them and those who hear and do them. The former shall be likened unto a foolish man who builds his house on the sand. It cannot withstand the storm, and great is the fall thereof. The latter is "likened unto a wise man, who built his house upon the rock: and the rain descended, and the floods came, and the winds blew, and beat upon that house; and it fell not: for it was founded upon the rock" (Matt. 7:24, 25).

When the Sermon on the Mount was ended, Jesus returned to Capernaum and was met by a Roman centurion who told Jesus that his faithful servant was lying at the point of death. As Jesus started toward the Roman officer's house, the centurion said to Him, "Lord, I am not worthy that thou shouldest come under my roof; but only say the word, and my servant shall be healed" (Matt. 8:8). Jesus was amazed and gratified by the man's remarkable faith and said, "Go thy way; as thou hast believed, *so* be it done unto thee" (Matt. 8:13). And the centurion's servant "was healed in that hour."

The healing of the officer's servant is another instance of "absent healing." The Roman centurion, though a man who had authority over others, was humble before Jesus, whose greatness he recognized and in whom he had faith. Our humility and faith pave the way for spiritual healing for ourselves and for our loved ones.

From Capernaum Jesus "went to a city called Nain; and his disciples went with him, and a great multitude" (Luke 7:11). As they entered the gate to the town a sad procession met their eyes. It was the funeral of a young man who was the only son of a widow.

And when the Lord saw her, he had compassion on her, and said unto her, Weep not. And he came nigh and touched the bier: and the bearers stood still. And he said, Young man, I say unto thee, Arise. And he that was dead sat up, and began to speak. And he gave him to his mother (Luke 7:13-15).

This is the first account we have of Jesus' raising the dead. He understood that life is eternal. He proved that the body can be reanimated by the realization of the omnipresent life of Spirit. Jesus "touched the bier," meaning that He contacted the death belief and filled it with life. We constantly meet death in various forms: death of faith, death of hope, death of ambition, and so on. Can we raise these error thoughts to life? To do so should be the goal of all Christians. Should we falter along the way, we will find strength and comfort in the Master's words: "Come unto me all ye that labor and are heavy laden, and I will give you rest. Take my yoke upon you, and learn of me (Matt. 11:28, 29).

Busy days followed in the life of the Master. The Pharisees were curious about Him, and one of them, Simon by name, invited Jesus to dine with him. While they were sitting at table, a woman "who was . . . a sinner" entered the room, bringing with her an alabaster cruse of ointment. "And standing behind at his feet, weeping, she began to wet his feet with her tears, and wiped them with the hair of her head, and kissed his feet, and anointed them with the ointment" (Luke 7:38). Simon thought that Jesus did not know what kind of woman she was, since the Master had allowed her to serve Him. It was the custom of the Pharisees to draw aside their robes when they met sinners. Then Jesus said to Simon:

A certain lender had two debtors: the one owed five hundred shillings, and the other fifty. When they had not *wherewith* to pay, he forgave them both. Which one of them therefore will love him most? (Luke 7:41-43).

Simon replied that the one who owed the most would feel the most loving. Then, pointing to the woman, Jesus remarked that she had treated Him with more love and respect than had Simon. "Where-

fore I say unto thee, Her sins; which are many, are
forgiven; for she loved much: but to whom little
is given, *the same* loveth little" (Luke 7:47-48).
Turning to the woman, Jesus said, "Thy sins are
forgiven. . . . Thy faith hath saved thee; go in
peace."

This incident serves to remind us that our trans-
gressions, even though they be of a serious nature,
are forgiven if we love that which is spiritual and
will turn from our wrongdoing to serve the Christ.

As Jesus journeyed through Galilee, stopping at
many villages, Mary Magdalene, from whom He
had formerly cast "seven devils" (mental obsessions); and Joanna, the wife of Chuza, Herod's
steward; Susanna, and many others ministered unto
Him. The Scriptures do not record when or where
the healing of Mary Magdalene took place. There is,
however, no authority to connect her with either the
sinful woman who washed the feet of Jesus at
Simon's house or the woman taken in adultery. Tradition has associated Mary Magdalene with one of
the two, and wrongly so. She is mentioned in the
Gospels as a woman whom Jesus healed, and who
later ministered to Him. She followed Him to the
Cross and was the first to whom He made Himself
known on the Resurrection morning.

The Pharisees were unable to understand Jesus'
ability to heal physical and mental illnesses. They
considered themselves more righteous than He; yet,
they could not perform healings similar to His.
When word was relayed to them that Jesus had

healed "one possessed with a demon, blind and dumb," they said, "This man doth not cast out demons, but by Beelzebub, the prince of the demons" (Matt. 12:24). Jesus replied that Satan cannot cast out Satan and that He healed "by the Spirit of God" (Matt. 12:28). Then He issued a stern warning:

Therefore I say unto you, Every sin and blasphemy shall be forgiven unto men; but the blasphemy against the Spirit shall not be forgiven. And whosoever shall speak a word against the Son of man, it shall be forgiven him; but whosoever shall speak against the Holy Spirit, it shall not be forgiven him (Matt. 12:31-33).

The "unforgivable sin," the speaking against the Holy Spirit, is our denial of the presence of God within us. When we think of ourselves as sick, poor, and miserable we are repudiating our true nature and denying the life and activity of the Holy Spirit in us. So long as we do this we cannot be forgiven. It is only by turning to God that we receive forgiveness. Whenever we will we may seek Him and be cleansed. But so long as we persistently turn from Him, deny Him, and maintain the errors of our ways, it is impossible for the forgiving love of our Father to be operative for us.

On one occasion as Jesus was teaching the multitudes, word was brought to Him that His mother and brothers wished to speak to Him:

But he answered and said unto him that told him, Who is my mother? and who are my brethren? And he stretched forth his hand towards his disciples, and said,

Behold, my mother and my brethren! For whosoever shall
do the will of my Father who is in heaven, he is my brother,
and sister, and mother (Matt. 12:48-50).

Here Jesus seems to deny the bond of blood relationships and to recognize only spiritual kinship.
This is a shortsighted view. Was He not giving us
a greater conception of kindred? The ties of common belief, aspiration, and work are as strong as
those of blood. Jesus' words give no ground for the
assumption that He refused to see His mother and
brothers or that He loved them less because He recognized a bond of kinship with His followers. He did
not overlook His obligation to His mother; even on
the Cross He made provision for her care. His re-
marks give us no justification for repudiating family
or relatives, but they do imply that we should en-
large the scope of our love to include persons who
are our friends and co-workers in the establishment
of a spiritual world.

During the second year of His ministry Jesus
gave His first great group of parables, though He
had already used the parabolic form of teaching to
some extent. A parable is a short, fictitious narrative
based on a familiar experience and having an application to spiritual life. Invariably Jesus took an
incident from everyday life to set forth a spiritual
truth. The parable was a favorite Jewish mode of
teaching, and Jesus imparted to it the richest and
most perfect development. These great parables of
Jesus included nine on the mysteries of the kingdom

of heaven or the kingdom of God. In the Gospel of Matthew, the phrase "kingdom of heaven" is used; whereas Mark and Luke use "kingdom of God." Both terms refer to the spiritual plane of man's being, which is the storehouse of divine ideas. Charles Fillmore says:

Jesus definitely located the kingdom of God (heaven) when He said, "The kingdom of God cometh not with observation: neither shall they say, Lo, here! or There! for lo, the kingdom of God is within you" (Luke 17:20, 21).

In order to find this kingdom, man must become conscious of Divine Mind and its realm of divine ideas, and be willing to adjust his thoughts to the divine standard.

Man adjusts his thought world to the kingdom of divine ideas through a process of denial by which he eliminates from consciousness all inharmonious ideas, and through affirmations of Truth by which he establishes himself in harmony with divine ideas.

Heaven is not confined to man's consciousness. It is everywhere present. When man's mind and body are in harmonious relation to divine ideas, his true thoughts flow into the realm of manifestation and bring forth the kingdom of the earth "as in heaven" (MD 387, 388).

To realize the kingdom within is the highest ideal man can set for himself. Each of the following parables gives a practical lesson on how to attain the consciousness of this inner kingdom.

"And all the multitude stood on the beach" (Matt. 13:2) as Jesus spoke various parables to them from a boat that was kept for Him on the Sea of Galilee for that purpose:

Parable of the Sower

(Matt. 13:3-9, 18-23)

"Behold, the sower went forth to sow." The sower is the indwelling Christ who is always speaking the word of Truth to men (sowing the seed). Four types of hearers are described. The first hears the word but is so lacking in spiritual understanding that his sense consciousness quickly obliterates it. The seeds "fell by the way side, and the birds came and devoured them." The second hears the word, receives it gladly, and remembers it for a time. However, he has only a superficial knowledge of Truth, and when trials come he thrusts the word aside. This hearer's mind is like the "rocky places, where they had not much earth." The sprouting seed, not having enough roots, is scorched by the sun's rays. The third hears the word, and his mind is like thorny ground. He is obsessed with a sense of burden ("the care of the world") and absorbed in the pursuit of wealth ("the deceitfulness of riches"). These are thorns that choke the seed and keep it from growing. The fourth hearer, as a result of his study of spiritual things and love for God, has a receptive mind. This represents the "good ground" that produces an abundant harvest. Each of us has the power to choose the kind of consciousness that he will have, and the outcome of our hearing the word will either be indifferent or beneficial, according to the way in which he receives it. The seed falls into our mind and responds to our consciousness.

Parable of the Growing Seed

(Mark 4:26-29)

In this parable Jesus teaches that our consciousness develops spiritually in the same mysterious way
that seeds do when planted in the ground. An idea
that is sown in the mind will grow if it receives the
nourishment and the encouragement it requires.
Understanding, faith, persistence, and application
allow divine ideas to unfold in an orderly manner:
"first the blade, then the ear, then the full grain
in the ear." We do not reap a harvest as soon as
the seed is sown; neither do we receive the entire
good we desire immediately after we plant divine
ideas in our consciousness. Our spiritual development, like physical development, is progressive, and
if we will be patient and faithful, we shall surely
come to the time of rich fulfillment.

Parable of the Tares

(Matt. 13:24-30, 36-43)

This parable has a particularly practical lesson
for us. It explains why there is a mixture of good
and evil in consciousness, even though our desire is
for good only. Through study and earnest prayer we
deliberately plant constructive thoughts (wheat),
yet, we are often dismayed when we find destructive
thoughts (tares) still lodging in our mind. The
tares are sown by the sense consciousness (enemy)
at times when we are not on the alert spiritually

("while men slept"). Our first impulse is to uproot
the tares immediately, that is, forcibly to dismiss
the destructive thoughts. This action would be unwise. It is better to "let both grow together until the
harvest." It would be difficult to cleanse our mind
thoroughly in the early stages of our spiritual development. If we attempted to do this, we may destroy much that is good along with the evil. When
we have attained sufficient spiritual understanding
(time of harvest), a separation can safely be made
and the good ideas preserved as the evil beliefs are
cast out.

Parable of the Mustard Seed

(Matt. 13:31, 32)

How does spiritual realization (the kingdom)
begin? Like all great accomplishments, it starts with
an idea. An initial divine idea is small amidst the
multitude of other thoughts in the mind. It is like a
tiny mustard seed sown in a field. Yet, an idea born
of Spirit has in it tremendous life and power. It
will grow until it becomes as strong and sturdy as
a tree and will serve as a lodging place for additional spiritual ideas ("the birds of the heaven").

Parable of the Leaven

(Matt. 13:33)

We must take deliberate action if we would
come into a higher realization of Truth. Even as it
is necessary to put leaven into bread if it is to be

fit to eat, so must we put the word of Truth into the conditions of our life if we are to express the good. Like the action of the leaven, our word does its work invisibly and silently. At first, we may be tempted to think that no progress is being made, but just as surely as the leaven caused the three measures of meal to rise, even so our word, spoken in faith, lifts our understanding to loftier heights. In due time, we become aware that a substantial and beneficial change has taken place and we realize that we have attained a great growth in consciousness.

Parable of the Hidden Treasure

(Matt. 13:44)

The teaching here is that we may discover Truth quite unexpectedly, just as a man digging in a field may, seemingly by chance, unearth a hidden treasure. For a time we keep this precious secret to ourselves and hide it in our heart. Eventually, however, we realize that if we are to have the benefit of God's good we must pay a price for it. The cost is our surrender to Him in time, devotion, and obedience ("selleth all that he hath"). Then the treasure is ours to be used to make life fuller and richer in every way.

Parable of the Pearl of Great Price

(Matt. 13:45, 46)

There is a marked similarity between this parable and the preceding one. In both there is the discovery

that Truth is the great good (treasure and pearl).
Sometimes this realization comes unexpectedly, as
in the parable of the hidden treasure, although in
this case it is the result of unconscious desire. In the
parable of the great pearl we are likened to the
merchant who is definitely seeking a better thing.
Our desire for it has become wholly conscious, and
we are persistent in our search. We have already accumulated much that is worth while (the merchant
had smaller gems) but we are not satisfied, for we
know that there is yet something greater to be acquired. Seeking, we shall surely find and we eventually come to understand that God is the ultimate
good. We then have located our great pearl. We
realize our oneness with God. Joyously we sever our
attachment to the lesser blessings that we have demonstrated, knowing that all our needs, both inner and
outer, are provided for.

Parable of the Net

(Matt. 13:47-50)

We live in a great sea of universal life. Our mind
accumulates every kind of thought, like a net that
has been "cast into the sea, and gathered of every
kind." When we come into an understanding of
Truth we have the discernment to separate good
ideas from limited beliefs. The ideas that increase
our spiritual stature are carefully preserved, and
the erroneous concepts that breed various kinds of
trouble are cast away.

The phrase "end of the world" that is used in this parable and in the parable of the tares does not mean a physical dissolution of the earth; it refers to the end of some phase of our own experience. A drastic change in our affairs marks the end of one world and the beginning of another. If we will ask for divine guidance at such a time, our spiritual ideas (angels) will overcome the vicious and destructive thoughts ("cast them into a furnace of fire"). Yet, these negative states of mind that belong to the race consciousness do not relinquish their hold on us without protest ("there shall be weeping and the gnashing of teeth"), and our salvation lies in our steadfastness in Truth.

When Jesus had finished the parable of the net He inquired of His hearers, "Have ye understood all these things?" Their affirmative answer brought forth His concluding parable:

Parable of the Householder

(Matt. 13:52)

As we hear, comprehend, and obey the word of Truth we become "a disciple in the kingdom of heaven" and are like a householder "who bringeth forth out of his treasure things new and old." Our treasure consists of all that goes to make up our spiritual consciousness. Part of it has been accumulated in the past. Every good thought and deed has made a contribution to righteousness, and this (the old) we retain. But spiritual unfoldment has no

ending, and as we listen to the Christ in us and understand His word realization on realization is added
(the new).

"And it came to pass, when Jesus finished these
parables, he departed thence" (Matt. 13:53). De-
ciding to cross the Sea of Galilee, Jesus and His
apostles entered a boat, and when they had set sail
Jesus fell asleep. After a time a storm arose. The
waves washed into the boat, and it began to fill with
water. The apostles were greatly frightened and
awoke Jesus, saying, "Teacher, carest thou not that
we perish?" (Mark 4:38).

And he awoke, and rebuked the wind, and said unto
the sea, Peace, be still. And the wind ceased and there was
a great calm. And he said unto them, "Why are ye fearful? have ye not yet faith? (Mark 4:39, 40).

This miracle shows the power that spiritual man
has even over the elements. The apostles represent
the human consciousness that is terrified by the
storm. The storm symbolizes any sort of threatening
occurrence in life. These men called to Jesus for
help. In times of stress we call on the Christ Spirit
within us. When the indwelling Christ is aroused by
our call, He takes charge, and the storm subsides.
Jesus then asked a question that we often ask ourselves, "Why are ye fearful? have ye not yet faith?"
We have seen the exercise of spiritual power; we
know that Truth works; yet when storms of various
kinds arise, we are fearful and our faith diminishes.
If we can remember to turn quickly to the Christ

(awaken Jesus), He will assume command and adjust matters. Then we shall be amazed at the might
of Spirit—"who then is this; that even the wind and
the sea obey him?" (Mark 4:41). Once more we
will view with awe and reverence the marvelous
works of the Son of God.

Up to this time, Jesus' ministry had been confined
almost entirely to Judea and Galilee. After He
crossed the Sea of Galilee He entered that section of
country known as the Decapolis, an area made up of
ten Greek cities, whose inhabitants were mostly Gentiles. This was Jesus' first journey to non-Jewish territory. On their arrival Jesus and His companions
were met by a man who is referred to as the Gera-
sene demoniac. Jesus had healed several such afflicted persons before, and He said, "Come forth,
thou unclean spirit, out of the man" (Mark 5:8).

In those days it was the common belief that an
insane person was possessed of demons with lives
and intelligence of their own, demons who resisted
all efforts to drive them from their abode in a person. The Bible records that the demons mentioned
in this incident recognized the power of Jesus which
could cast them out, and they implored Him to send
them into a herd of swine grazing on the mountain-
side. "And he gave them leave. And the unclean
spirits came out, and entered into the swine; and
the herd rushed down the steep into the sea . . .
and they were drowned in the sea" (Mark 5:13).

This incident about the demoniac is perhaps one
of the most obscure passages in the Bible, and any

attempt to interpret it literally is well nigh impossible. "The Abingdon Bible Commentary" (Page 1006) gives a brief explanation:

It would seem that Jesus on this first visit of His to the Decapolis . . . met a man suffering from the delusion that he was possessed of a legion of evil spirits. After some conversation with him Jesus was able to deliver him from the delusion and restore him to mental health.

But what is the spiritual significance of the event? With regard to demons Charles Fillmore states:

Demons, or evil spirits, are conditions of mind, or states of consciousness, that have been developed because the creative power of man has been used in an unwise or an ignorant way. . . . The mind builds states of consciousness that become established in brain and body. Both good and evil are found in the unregenerate man, but in the new birth evil and all its works must be cast out. The work of every overcomer is to cast out of himself the demons of sin and evil, through the power and dominion of his indwelling Christ (MD 170).

Adverse states of consciousness (demons) are tenacious and do not relinquish their hold easily. When their rule is threatened by our determined efforts to be rid of them, they seek other habitats or places of residence in consciousness. For example, we may have allowed excessive fears as regards some condition in our body to take root in our mind. When these fears are about to be "cast out" as a result of prayer, they are quite likely to seek expression in some other circumstances of our life. Swine are unclean animals and represent sensuous, impure thoughts. In this healing the demons left the man at the command of Jesus and entered the swine. This means that obsessions that are dislodged at one point in consciousness find temporary refuge in some other phase of the carnal nature. As the herd rushed into the sea and perished, so evil is ultimately destroyed if we will be faithful in focusing our thought energy on the indwelling Christ and claim union with Him.

CHAPTER VII

Clouds of Opposition

(Second Year)

AFTER JESUS VISITED the territory of the Gera-
senes He returned to His headquarters in
Capernaum, where He was met by Jairus,
a ruler of the synagogue. Jairus beseeched Jesus to
come to his home to heal his young daughter, who
was critically ill. Jesus immediately responded, but
the great crowds that followed Him slowed His
progress.

And a woman, who had an issue of blood twelve years,
and had suffered many things of many physicians, and had
spent all that she had, and was nothing bettered, but rather
grew worse, having heard the things concerning Jesus,
came in the crowd behind, and touched his garment. For
she said, If I touch but his garments, I shall be made
whole. And straightway the fountain of her blood was
dried up; and she felt in her body that she was healed of
her plague. (Mark 5:25-29).

This incident is one of the great lessons on faith.
The woman had been ill for a long time, yet, she
had not given up hope of regaining her health.
When she heard of the remarkable cures that Jesus
had effected, she made a determined effort to reach
Him by pushing through the crowd. Her faith was
so strong that she believed she would recover, even
if she only touched the hem of His garment.

Healing comes when we make contact with the

Christ, whom Jesus represents. We need to come boldly before the throne of grace and push through the "crowd" that separates us from our Christ self, our own destructive thoughts and feelings. Our part is to be persistent in making our way through them. Jesus said that it was the woman's faith which brought about her healing, and faith also brings healing to us. If we believe that it is God's will for us to be well, we will not let anything keep us from contacting the Christ and receiving wholeness from Him.

While Jesus was speaking to the woman who had touched His garment, word was brought to Jairus that his daughter had died and that there was no need for Jesus to come.

But Jesus hearing it, answered him, Fear not: only believe, and she shall be made whole. And when he came to the house, he suffered not any man to enter in with him, save Peter, and John, and James, and the father of the maiden and her mother. And all were weeping, and bewailing her: but he said, Weep not; for she is not dead, but sleepeth. And they laughed him to scorn, knowing that she was dead. But he, taking her by the hand, called, saying, Maiden, arise. And her spirit returned, and she rose up immediately: and he commanded that *something* be given her to eat (Luke 8:50-55).

This was the second instance where Jesus raised a dead person, and it is recorded in sufficient detail for us to understand the steps that He took in performing the miracle. When He entered the home He shut out the multitude, but took Peter (faith),

James (judgment), John (love), and the parents with Him. The three statements Jesus made contain the secret of a quickening from death to life. First, He said to the child's father, "Fear not: only believe, and she shall be made whole." Fear must be dismissed from consciousness and replaced with a steadfast faith. Second, He denied the reality of death: "She is not dead, but sleepeth." The life of God that gives animation to the body always exists. Then He spoke directly to the Christ life within the child and said to her, "Maiden, arise." The word spoken in faith brings about a restoration.

As Jesus departed from the home of Jairus, two blind men followed Him and begged to be healed. He asked, "Believe ye that I am able to do this?" When they replied in the affirmative, He touched their eyes, and they were opened.

"And Jesus strictly charged them, saying, See that no man know it" (Matt. 9:30).

On several occasions Jesus told persons whom He had healed not to speak about their healings. There is a definite reason for this. In telling of a spiritual healing, a person speaks also of the limitation that has been overcome, and it is easy for the mind to slip back into the consciousness of the limitation. This is likely to bring about a return of the troublesome condition. It is best to give thanks for the healing and then give full attention to right living in the present. A person is justified in telling of a demonstration only when his doing so will serve to inspire another's faith.

Jesus then returned to Nazareth. He had not been back to His home town since He had spoken in the synagogue there at the beginning of His Galilean ministry, at which time He had aroused the enmity of the Jewish leaders. This was before His fame had become so widespread. On this second visit these leaders still resented Him. Was He not simply a carpenter, the son of Mary, whose family resided among them?

And Jesus said unto them, A prophet is not without honor, save in his own country, and among his own kin, and in his own house. And he could there do no mighty work, save that he laid his hands upon a few sick folk, and healed them. And he marvelled because of their unbelief (Mark 6:3-6).

It is sometimes difficult to believe that what is so close to us has any outstanding value. "Distance lends enchantment" is a true adage. We are loath to acknowledge the Christ within, for we seem to be such commonplace persons. Because we do not fully believe in the mighty power that is "closer . . . than breathing," we too often close the door to the good that Spirit would gladly bestow. Jesus was astonished that the people whom He knew intimately could not accept Him. However, others did accept Him, and great crowds followed Him wherever He went. Yet the friends whom He longed to help had no faith in Him, and He was powerless to help them. Without our faith and willingness to receive, the Christ Spirit cannot move through us to bring blessings.

This second rebuff separated Jesus from the village of His childhood, and He never returned to Nazareth again. Instead, He went throughout the cities and towns of Galilee, "teaching in their synagogues, and preaching the gospel of the kingdom, and healing all manner of disease and all manner of sickness" (Matt. 9:35).

During His third tour of Galilee, Jesus was moved with compassion when He saw the multitudes that followed Him. They reminded Him of sheep without a shepherd, of a harvest that is ripe but unreaped for lack of laborers. He bade His apostles pray to the Lord of the harvest that He would send forth laborers into His fields. Each of us should pray that he may be worthy to be used by the Father in serving Him and bringing His abundant good into manifestation.

Immediately after He had traversed the whole of Galilee, Jesus sent His apostles "to the lost sheep of the house of Israel." He sent them two by two, to confirm His teaching and to heal in His name:

And as ye go, preach, saying, The kingdom of heaven is at hand. Heal the sick, raise the dead, cleanse the lepers, cast out demons; freely ye received freely give (Matt. 10:7, 8).

This is the work of the Christian disciple today. If we are to enter into the Christ consciousness, we must begin now to do His work in our own consciousness. Our preaching should concern the immediacy of the kingdom; that is, we should tell ourselves over and over again that God is good and that God is here. We should heal the sick thoughts, cleanse the leprous or unclean emotions, and cast out the mean and corrupt states of mind. We have received freely from God, who gave us of Himself. We should give freely of our spiritual resources to the unredeemed forces of our being.

As we are lifted in consciousness, the time comes when we are also to serve outwardly. But as we go forth in His name,

Get you no gold, nor silver, nor brass in your purses; no wallet for *your* journey, neither two coats, nor shoes, nor staff: for the laborer is worthy of his food (Matt. 10:9, 10).

Material things do not give us the power to accomplish; yet a firm and steadfast consciousness coupled with a burning desire to do His work does supply this power. We do not need gold so much as we need ideas. Our physical needs will be provided as we serve Him faithfully.

Behold, I send you forth as sheep in the midst of wolves: be ye therefore wise as serpents, and harmless as doves. But beware of men: for they will deliver you up to councils, and in their synagogues they will scourge you; yea and before governors and kings shall ye be brought for my sake, for a testimony to them and to the Gentiles. But when they deliver you up, be not anxious how or what ye shall speak: for it shall be given you in that hour what ye shall speak. For it is not ye that speak, but the Spirit of your Father that speaketh in you (Matt. 10:16-21).

The path of spiritual service, whether in the
home, the business world, or the ministry, has its
hazards, as does every other meritorious endeavor.
Jesus did not say that the way is easy, but He did say
that it is worth while and that we should not fear
malicious power in the outer world. We will know
what to say when we are attacked or persecuted for
our convictions, because the Father whom we are
serving will speak through us. There may be times
when we are delivered up to our enemies, outer
forces that seem mightier than we are, but we have
Jesus' assurance of protection.

Think not that I came to send peace on the earth: I
came not to send peace, but a sword. For I came to set
a man at variance against his father, and the daughter
against her mother, and the daughter in law against her
mother in law: and a man's foes *shall be* they of his own
household. . . . And he that doth not take his cross and
follow after me, is not worthy of me. He that findeth his
life shall lose it; and he that loseth his life for my sake
shall find it (Matt. 10:34-39).

Jesus' words as regards peace will likely startle us
when we first read them. Was He not the Prince
of Peace? We should take into consideration that
there are two kinds of peace: one is destructive, and
the other is constructive. Peace at any price, which
means the surrender of one's highest beliefs to appease another, is destructive. Jesus did not advocate
this sort of peace. Peace that results from our sense
of oneness with God is constructive, and Jesus referred to this when He said, "Peace I leave with

you; my peace I give unto you: not as the world giveth, give I unto you. Let not your heart be troubled, neither let it be fearful" (John 14:27). Such is an inward peace, the peace of God. It can function in the very midst of turmoil.

Jesus' declaration that He came not to send peace but a sword was made to His intimate friends, the apostles, who were going out to do His works. He warned them not to compromise His teachings for the sake of popularity. His words were like a sword that would cut through the erroneous beliefs of men, and His apostles would not be liked.

We must be prepared for a conflict between old human concepts and new spiritual ideas. The latter are higher than beliefs that are entertained by the sense mind, and for a time the clash of the two causes an agitation in consciousness. This is a part of our spiritual progress, and we should not fear it. Truth is sharp like a sword and cuts through the states of mind that we no longer desire and know that we do not need.

The restricting thoughts that are resident in the personal consciousness are our only enemies, for "a man's foes *shall be* they of his own household." These thoughts must be crossed out if we are to be worthy of our high calling, which is to follow Him. The person who makes material things the aim and object of his existence, or who finds a full life in worldly pursuits, loses his capacity for spiritual expression, which is his real life. On the other hand, the person who is willing to lose outer gain for the attainment of spiritual understanding and service ("loseth his life for my sake") will enjoy the more abundant life of Spirit.

During the absence of the apostles on their missionary tour, Jesus continued His work. Herod Antipas, the ruler of Galilee, heard reports of what Jesus was doing and was exceedingly fearful. Herod had considered John a religious fanatic, and he considered Jesus of the same caliber. "This is John the Baptist; he is risen from the dead" (Matt. 14:2) Herod exclaimed, and he sought to see Jesus. But Jesus, who had heard of the cruel and senseless slaying of John the Baptist, departed from Galilee as soon as the apostles returned. "Come ye yourselves apart into a desert place, and rest a while" (Mark 6:31). This was Jesus' invitation to them. However, many persons, seeing them leave, followed Jesus to the east coast of the Sea of Galilee. He had compassion on them and instead of resting, He taught the multitude all day.

The crowd of five thousand listened eagerly. When night began to fall the apostles suggested that Jesus send them into the nearby villages to find food. "For we are here in a desert place," they said (Luke 9:12). Instead, Jesus commanded the apostles to feed the multitude, which seemed impossible to them, as they could find only five loaves and two fishes:

And he [Jesus] took the five loaves and two fishes, and looking up to heaven, he blessed them, and brake; and gave to the disciples to set before the multitude. And they ate, and were all filled: and there was taken up that which remained over to them of broken pieces, twelve baskets (Luke 9:16, 17).

This is a very spectacular miracle, and many efforts have been made by sincere Christians to explain it in terms of human possibility. Some have advanced the theory that the people who heard Jesus that day were so filled with spiritual nourishment that they felt no need for food. Others have said that many of His hearers had food with them and shared it with others. Unity accepts the miracle literally, for it is clear evidence of the ability of spiritual man (Jesus Christ) to mold the ever-present substance and bring it into manifestation. Charles Fillmore states:

The origin or source of all substance is the *idea* of substance. It is purely spiritual and can be apprehended only by the mind. It is never visible to the eye, nor can it be sensed by man through any of the bodily faculties. . . .

When the mind has centered its attention upon this idea of substance long enough and strongly enough, it generates the consciousness of substance, and through the powers of the various faculties of the mind in right relation it can form visible substance. Jesus in this way brought into visibility the loaves and fishes to feed the five thousand (MJ 73, 74).

The details that are given on this miracle of feeding the multitude contain a practical and helpful lesson in demonstration for us. The apostles and the crowd represent the human way of viewing things. To them there was no possibility of finding food for the multitude on the arid plain where they were. Oftentimes we find ourselves in conditions that seem just as barren but we can train ourselves to remember that even in such conditions there is much that is available if only we know how to bring it forth. Here is a concise formula for the demonstration of substance. Jesus looked to heaven by fixing His attention on spiritual substance, the source of abundance. He did not think about lack. He thought about abundance, and then thanked God for the supply at hand. To praise our Lord and to give thanks for what we have is the surest way to increase our supply. If we have a little health or a little supply, we can add to it by praise and thanksgiving. Gratitude opens our consciousness to receive more. A supply of good is always available, for God is omnipresent. Jesus broke the five loaves and the two fishes and gave the pieces to the apostles to distribute to the multitude. This shows that we are to use what we have, though it be but a small amount. If we use what we have wisely, we make room for more. If muscles are not exercised they become flabby. If we have only a small amount of money and hoard it, we shut off the possibilities of gaining more. The law is that we must give, and we shall then receive. There is never a lack of good. There is only a lack of realization on our part that God's limitless substance is available to His children.

The miracle of the loaves and fishes so impressed the people that they wanted to make Jesus a king (John 6:14, 15). Such was not His desire. Perceiving their intention, He withdrew to a mountain to pray, having first instructed the apostles to go on ahead of Him to Capernaum.

Entering their boat, the apostles started across the Sea of Galilee. Soon a storm arose. When it was at the height of its fury, they saw a figure walking toward them on the water. They cried out in fear, thinking that it was an apparition. Then a voice sounded through the darkness, saying, "It is I; be not afraid" (Matt. 14:27), and they recognized it as the voice of their beloved Master:

And Peter answered him and said, Lord, if it be thou, bid me come unto thee upon the waters. And he said, Come. And Peter went down from the boat and walked upon the waters to come to Jesus. But when he saw the wind, he was afraid; and beginning to sink, he cried out, saying, Lord, save me. And immediately Jesus stretched forth his hand, and took hold of him, and saith unto him, O thou of little faith, wherefore didst thou doubt (Matt. 14:28-31)?

Peter represents faith, and faith dares to do that which seems impossible. Believing that he could also walk on the water at Jesus' command, Peter started toward the Master. However, before he reached Jesus his attention was distracted by the storm and he became fearful. As soon as fear entered his consciousness, Peter began to sink. There are times when we have the faith to begin projects; yet, when obstacles arise we falter. When we begin to sink, will we remember to do what Peter did? He called to Jesus, and Jesus immediately held out His hand to the wavering apostle. Perhaps from this very experience, Peter learned the lesson that enabled him to say to the crowd on the Day of Pentecost, "Whosoever shall call on the name of the Lord shall be saved" (Acts 2:21).

The people who had eaten the loaves and fishes that Jesus had multiplied and who wanted to make Him king lost Him overnight, but they finally located Him the next morning in Capernaum. Jesus knew that they followed Him not for the spiritual teaching He gave but because they "ate of the loaves and were filled." He admonished them, "Work not for the food which perisheth, but for the food which abideth unto eternal life, which the Son of man shall give unto you: for him the Father, *even* God, hath sealed" (John 6:27).

This is the beginning of Jesus' great teaching that is known as the Discourse on the Bread of Life and is recorded in the 6th chapter of John. The people wanted to know how they might do the "works of God," and Jesus replied, "This is the work of God, that ye believe on him whom he hath sent" (John 6:29). We are to believe in the indwelling Christ whom God has given us. The people then requested a sign from Him that they might believe. They said their ancestors had eaten the bread from heaven, the manna that fell when Moses prayed. Could not Jesus then give them a similar sign? Jesus replied, "It was not Moses that gave you the bread out of heaven; but my Father giveth you the true bread out of heaven." They asked for this bread, and Jesus said:

I am the bread of life: he that cometh to me shall not hunger, and he that believeth on me shall never thirst. But I said unto you, that ye have seen me, and yet believe not. All that which the Father giveth me shall come unto me; and him that cometh to me I will in no wise cast out. For I am come down from heaven, not to do mine own will, but the will of him that sent me. And this is the will of him that sent me, that of all that which he hath given me I shall lose nothing, but should raise it up at the last day. For this is the will of my Father, that every one that beholdeth the Son, and believeth on him, should have eternal life (John 6:35-40).

The Spirit of God in us, the Christ, is our source of nourishment, our bread of life. When we believe in and trust the Christ self as it is revealed to us, we attain an awareness of the eternal life which is of God. Charles Fillmore states:

All shall attain who believe or have faith in the spiritual source of life. Whoever comes to this Christ realm in the heavens all about us will be moved by its will, which is the will of the Father. There will be no loss, no failure in this realm, and whoever enters into this Mind of Spirit will have poured out to him its life essence and be wholly raised up from material conditions when arriving at the "last day" (the last degree of understanding) (MJ 74, 75).

Jesus' words on the true bread sounded very strange to the listening Jews. They were shocked and began to take exception to what He said. They questioned, as others also had questioned: Was not this man the son of Joseph, and had they not known His parents? How could He say that He came down out of heaven? Jesus warned:

Verily, verily, I say unto you, He that believeth hath
eternal life. I am the bread of life. Your fathers ate the
manna in the wilderness, and they died. This is the bread
which cometh down out of heaven, that a man may eat
thereof, and not die. I am the living bread which came
down out of heaven: if any man eat of this bread, he shall
live for ever: yea and the bread which I will give is my
flesh, for the life of the world (John 6:47-51).

The Jews could not comprehend how Jesus could
give them His flesh to eat. But He insisted: "Except
ye eat the flesh of the Son of man and drink his
blood, ye have not life in yourselves. . . . For my flesh
is meat indeed, and my blood is drink indeed. He
that eateth my flesh and drinketh my blood abideth
in me, and I in him" (John 6:53-56). Jesus was here
foreshadowing the teaching that He was to give
later at the Last Supper when He instituted what we
now call the Communion. The body (flesh) and
blood of Jesus represent the substance and life of
Christ. When our minds appropriate this idea of
divine substance and divine life, we symbolically are
eating His flesh and drinking His blood.

To many who had followed Jesus up to this time,
His words were a "hard saying." They could not
believe, and "walked no more with him."

Many people start out to walk in the light of Spirit,
to unfold Truth, but they become entangled in their own
misgivings and disbelief and therefore return to their old
limited way of life (MJ 76).

We can imagine how Jesus must have felt when
He turned to the Twelve and asked, "Would ye also

go away?" Peter replied: "Lord, to whom shall we go? thou hast the words of eternal life. And we have believed and know that thou art the Holy One of God" (John 6:68-70). Stanch and courageous words these! It is sometimes difficult for us to understand and believe the deep things that are revealed by Spirit. Yet, when faith (Peter) has been quickened in consciousness, we know that Spirit is the only one to whom we can turn: there is no other source that can give us the words of eternal life. Such occasions are testing times for those of us who are on the spiritual path. If we affirm our faith in Christ, we gain strength, and the seeming mysteries are clarified.

This particular teaching utterly crushed the hopes of persons who looked to Jesus as a political Messiah to whose cause they could rally. His words were abhorrent to the orthodox Jews. Many whom He had healed and helped still loved Him even though they did not understand, but these constituted a small minority. From this time Jesus' cause in Galilee seemed doomed.

Shortly after Jesus gave His Discourse on the Bread of Life, another incident occurred that deepened the rift between Him and the Jews. Some scribes and Pharisees from Jerusalem had observed that Jesus' apostles ate without washing their hands in the prescribed manner. They were violating the oral tradition, and its regulations were extremely elaborate and numerous. Before every meal and at every return from market a Jew was commanded to wash. If there were no water at hand, he was obliged to go at least four miles to search for it. In addition, there were rules for the washing of all cups, banquet couches, and brazen vessels, and no less than twenty-six prayers accompanied these tasks. "Why do thy disciples transgress the tradition of the elders?" they asked (Matt. 15:2). Instead of answering, Jesus put a question to them: "Why do ye also transgress the commandment of God because of your tradition?" (Matt. 15:3) He reminded them that God commands a man to honor his father and mother, yet, the scribes made a rule that if a person gave into the Temple treasury the sum that was intended for his parents, he did not have to support them. The scribes twisted a good law for their own benefit, yet, they assumed a self-righteous attitude that concerned the breaking of a tradition that had no real value.

And he [Jesus] called to him the multitude, and said unto them, Hear, and understand: Not that which entereth into the mouth defileth the man; but that which proceedeth out of the mouth, this defileth the man (Matt. 15:10, 11).

It is not the outer observance of religious forms that is of importance, but what is in the heart of a person. If evil is in the heart, the mouth speaks it, and that which comes out of the heart is what defiles a man. To hide their corruptness, the Jewish leaders put emphasis on trifling details. Jesus knew that the leadership they furnished would lead the people to ruin. "They are blind guides," He said, "And if the blind guide the blind, both shall fall into a pit" (Matt. 15:14).

Throughout the second year of His ministry, Jesus had preached and healed, principally in Galilee; moving among the people and seizing every opportunity to instruct and help them. His words and great works attracted widespread attention, and for a time it seemed that the Galileans would follow Him. By the end of the year, however, it became evident that this was not to be. The Pharisees had become increasingly resentful of Jesus, and they had great influence over the masses. Jesus had antagonized the Pharisees by dishonoring many things they had been taught to regard as sacred. They should be pitied more than blamed, for they were spiritually blind. Their own hard and fast rules closed their eyes to any improvements in religion, and they considered Jesus to be a deceiver of the people. At first He had attempted to explain His ideas, but the Pharisees were unconvinced. When He continued His ministry in spite of their objections, they grew to hate Him. They did everything they could to turn the people against Him, and when the tide of His popularity began to wane at the end of His second year of ministry, they took advantage of this and attacked Him more viciously.

The conflict between Jesus and the Pharisees represents the inevitable clash between the sense man and the spiritual consciousness:

For my thoughts are not your thoughts, neither are your ways my ways, saith Jehovah. For as the heavens are higher than the earth, so are my ways higher than your ways, and my thoughts than your thoughts (Isa. 55:8, 9).

CHAPTER VIII

Crucifixion and Resurrection Foretold

(Third Year)

TO ALL APPEARANCES the Pharisees had gained the upper hand temporarily. Perceiving that little could be accomplished in Galilee, Jesus and His apostles journeyed to Tyre and Sidon, cities of Phœnicia.

It was during Jesus' sojourn in Phœnicia that the healing of the daughter of a Syrophœnician woman took place (Matt. 15:21-28). The mother was a Gentile, and when she asked Jesus for help, He replied, "I was not sent but unto the lost sheep of the house of Israel" (Matt. 15:24). Literally, His words mean that, as a Jew, He felt that His ministry should be to His own race. It was not until after the Resurrection that He commanded the apostles, "Go ye into all the world, and preach the gospel to the whole creation" (Mark 16:15). The spiritual significance of Jesus' words to the Gentile woman is that Gentiles represent the worldly mind, but Jews (Children of Israel) represent the mind that is turned toward God. Only persons who have some love for and understanding of Truth can receive spiritual enlightenment. However, the mother persisted in her plea, showing that faith was awakening in her. To Jesus' objection, "It is not meet to take the children's bread and cast it to the dogs," which means that it is wise to use care in sharing spiritual things with those still in the depths of mortal consciousness, the woman replied, "Yea, Lord; for even the dogs eat of the crumbs which fall from their masters' table." Though she knew she was unworthy, she believed that Jesus would help her. Her humility and faith aroused Jesus' compassion, and He commended her, saying, "O woman, great is thy faith: be it done unto thee even as thou wilt. And her daughter was healed from that hour." Even though we may still be functioning largely on the plane of mortal thought, a humble faith in God enables us to receive His good.

From Phœnicia Jesus and His apostles went again to the Decapolis, east of the Jordan River. On their arrival a deaf and dumb man was brought to Jesus.

And he took him aside from the multitude privately, and put his fingers into his ears, and he spat, and touched his tongue; and looking up to heaven, he sighed, and saith unto him, Ephphatha, that is, Be opened. And his ears were opened, and the bond of his tongue was loosed, and he spake plain (Mark 7:33-35).

This healing is one of the few instances in which Jesus combined physical action with speaking the word, and it serves as a reminder to us that though we are receiving physical help, we should also seek God through prayer.

As He had done on previous occasions, Jesus asked that the healing of the deaf and dumb man be kept secret, but the people who had seen it were so astonished that they told it abroad. As a consequence, great multitudes followed Jesus to the summit of a hill overlooking the Sea of Galilee. There they brought the lame, the blind, and the maimed to the Great Physician, and He healed them all.

For three days Jesus stayed with them, teaching and healing. So great were the crowds that gathered to hear His teaching that their food supply ran out. Once more He fed a multitude (four thousand) with seven loaves and a few small fishes (Mark 8:1-9).

A different reception awaited Jesus on His return to Galilee. In contrast to the enthusiasm and gratitude of the people in the Decapolis, He was met by a group of Pharisees and Sadducees, who demanded "a sign from heaven" (Matt. 16:1). Up to this time the Sadducees, who were not deeply religious, had shown little interest in Jesus' ministry. Their interests were largely political. On this occasion, however, they joined the Pharisees in questioning Him. The latter had already discovered that the most effective weapon that could be used to discredit Jesus was to ask for a "sign." If He were the Son of God, as He claimed to be, surely He could give them some spectacular performance that would prove His claim. They discounted His great healings by saying that He was in league with Beelzebub and they knew by this time that He would not perform any great feats to satisfy their curiosity. However, His consistent refusal gave them opportunities to poison the people's minds against Him. His reply to their demand for a sign was:

When it is evening ye say, *It will be* fair weather: for the heaven is red. And in the morning, *It will be* foul weather to-day; for the heaven is red and lowering. Ye know how to discern the face of the heaven; but ye cannot *discern* the signs of the times (Matt. 16:2, 3).

The Pharisees and Sadducees could indeed read certain signs, but they could not see that the Messiah for whom they longed was in their midst. We must believe before we can discern the works of Jesus Christ.

Do you ask for a sign of power? Do you want miraculous healing without fulfilling the law of right thinking and right doing? Then you are not receiving the Christ Spirit rightly. You are seeking the temporal instead of the eternal, and if you let this superficial phase of mind rule, you will reject the Christ Spirit and cast it out of your midst (MD 347).

Jesus left Galilee and went to Cæsarea Philippi. No hostility had been aroused toward Him there, and it was His intention to quietly instruct the Twelve. As He crossed the Sea of Galilee Jesus cautioned His companions to "beware of the leaven of the Pharisees and Sadducees" (Matt. 16:6). His companions understood that He wanted them to shun the false teaching of these religious leaders so that it would not come into their consciousness where it might expand unawares.

At the outskirts of the little village of Bethsaida, a blind man was brought to Jesus. This is the one recorded case of a partial healing followed by a complete healing. Jesus laid His hands on the blind man's eyes and asked, "Seest thou aught?" (Mark 8:23). The man said, "I see men; for I behold *them* as trees, walking." This indicates that although he could distinguish figures, his vision was distorted. Jesus again touched him, and clear vision was restored. This should encourage us to be grateful for any improvement in conditions about which we are praying. If we will continue to "pray through," the full healing will come.

Now when Jesus came into the parts of Cæsarea Philippi, he asked his disciples, saying, Who do men say that the Son of man is? And they said, Some *say* John the Baptist; some, Elijah; and others, Jeremiah, or one of the prophets. He saith unto them, But who say ye that I am? And Simon Peter answered and said, Thou art the Christ, the Son of the living God. And Jesus answered and said unto him, Blessed art thou, Simon Bar-Jonah: for flesh and blood hath not revealed it unto thee, but my Father which is in heaven. And I also say unto thee, that thou art Peter, and upon this rock I will build my church; and the gates of Hades shall not prevail against it (Matt. 16:13-18).

By this question Jesus was testing the spiritual understanding of His apostles. They represent the twelve spiritual faculties or powers of man, and it is the faith faculty (Peter) who declares, "Thou art the Christ." Jesus said that this revelation comes by faith, not by human sense ("flesh and blood"), but by the Spirit of God that dwells in man ("my Father which is in heaven"). Charles Fillmore states:

This revealment of Truth direct from Spirit is the rock upon which the one and only church of Jesus Christ is built. All other authorities are spurious (TT 103).

He says further:

The true church of Christ is a state of consciousness in man, but few have gone so far in the realization as to know that in the very body of each man and woman is a temple in which the Christ holds religious services at all times: "Ye are a temple of God." The appellation is not symbolical, but a statement of architectural truth. Under the direction of the Christ, a new body is constructed by the thinking faculty in man; the materials entering into this superior structure are the spiritualized organic substances, and the new creation is the temple or body of Spirit" (TT 105).

To Peter (faith) Jesus gave "the keys of the kingdom of heaven: and whatsoever thou shalt bind on earth shall be bound in heaven: and whatsoever thou shalt loose on earth shall be loosed in heaven" (Matt. 16:19). As regards this teaching, Mr. Fillmore says:

That Peter today stands at the gate of heaven is no mere figure of speech; he always stands there when you have acknowledged the Christ, and he has the "keys of the kingdom of heaven." The keys are the thoughts that he forms, the words that he speaks. He then stands porter at the door of thought and freely exercises that power which the Christ declares: "Whatsoever thou shalt bind on earth shall be bound in heaven . . . "

You can see readily why this faith-thinker, Peter, is the foundation; why the faith faculty should be guarded, di-

rected, and trained. His words are operative on many
planes of consciousness, and he will bind you to conditions
of servitude if you do not guard his acts closely.

Persons who let their thinking faculty attach itself to
the things of earth are limiting or binding their free ideas,
or "heaven," and they thereby become slaves to hard, material conditions, gradually shutting out any desire for
higher things.

Those who look right through the apparent hardships
of earthly environments and persistently declare them not
material, but spiritual, are loosing them in the ideal or
"heaven," and such conditions must, through the creative
power vested in the thinker, eventually rearrange themselves according to his word (MD 517).

Jesus then began to prepare His apostles for His
trial in Jerusalem. "The Son of man must suffer
many things, and be rejected of the elders and chief
priests and scribes, and be killed, and the third day
be raised up" (Luke 9:22). They did not understand Him. Peter took exception to what He said,
"Be it far from thee, Lord: this shall never be unto
thee" (Matt. 16:22). But Jesus rebuked the impetuous Peter, "Get thee behind me, Satan: thou
art a stumbling-block unto me: for thou mindest not
the things of God, but the things of men" (Matt.
16:23). Jesus realized that the time was not far distant when He would be assailed outwardly; yet He
knew that He was making the overcoming within
Himself and that His death would be followed by
His resurrection. This was incomprehensible to the
apostles. They believed Him to be the Messiah, an
all-powerful ruler, and they could not believe that

His enemies were strong enough to overthrow Him. The apostles reasoned that Jesus' statements about His future must be parabolic utterances that referred to the end of His present lowly position with the coming of a far better and glorious position. On several occasions when Jesus talked of the Cross, the apostles still did not understand. They discussed His words among themselves but, not realizing the spiritual significance of them, they became ambitious and, sensing a change, they sought positions for themselves in the new regime they were convinced would be established.

It is difficult for the human mind to perceive that spiritual mastery is the one goal worth striving for, and that it demands the complete surrender of self. Man must be willing to give up natural inclinations before he can take on spiritual characteristics. Jesus knew this. It was the way He had chosen, and nothing could deter Him. Yet He seemed unable to convey His intention even to those who were closest to Him. He warned them that He would be attacked, but they were not to be ashamed of Him, for He would come into the glory of the Father. Furthermore, "I tell you a truth, There are some of them that stand here, who shall in no wise taste of death, till they see the kingdom of God" (Luke 9:27). And indeed, the apostles did see the kingdom when the Holy Spirit came on them at Pentecost.

The Twelve were soon to have a preview of the Master's glory. Leaving Cæsarea Philippi, they journeyed north toward Mount Hermon. There Jesus went to the mountain to pray, taking with Him Peter, James, and John.

And as he was praying, the fashion of his countenance was altered, and his raiment *became* white and dazzling. And behold, there talked with him two men, which were Moses and Elijah; who appeared in glory, and spake of his decease which he was about to accomplish at Jerusalem. Now Peter and they that were with him were heavy with sleep: but when they were fully awake, they saw his glory, and the two men that stood with him. And it came to pass, as they were parting from him, Peter said unto Jesus, Master, it is good for us to be here: and let us make three tabernacles; one for thee, and one for Moses, and one for Elijah: not knowing what he said. And while he said these things, there came a cloud, and overshadowed them: and they feared as they entered into the cloud. And a voice came out of the cloud, saying, This is my Son, my chosen: hear ye him. And when the voice came, Jesus was found alone (Luke 9:29-36).

The value of the Transfiguration is in its symbolic meaning. Jesus Himself referred to it as a vision and told the apostles not to speak of it until after His resurrection (Matt. 17:9). Since He was sustained by faith (Peter), judgment (James), and love (John), He attained such a high state of consciousness that light shone from Him and about Him. With Jesus, representing the Christ, were the law (Moses) and the prophetic utterances (Elijah). Obedience to the truths given by the law and the prophets is the process by which we rise to the Christ consciousness. Faith (Peter) is so impressed by the spectacle that it wants to preserve the vision in concrete form (build three tabernacles). This is prompt-ly rejected by the voice or inspiration of God call-ing attention to His Son and commanding, "Hear ye him."

Of the Transfiguration Charles Fillmore states:

Transfiguration is always preceded by a change of mind. Our ideas must be lifted from the material, the phys-ical, to the spiritual. But first we need to realize that it is possible for us to be transfigured as well as to understand the law by which transfiguration is brought about. . . .

In our study and application of the Christian life we all have times when we are spiritually uplifted. Such a time is marked by a form of spiritual enthusiasm, which is brought about by statements of Truth made by ourselves or others—prayers, words of praise, songs, meditations—any statement of Truth that exalts the spiritual realms of the mind. Jesus was lifted up by Peter, James, and John (faith, judgment, and love). Whenever we dwell upon these virtues and try to live up to them, they are exalted in consciousness, and they go with us to the mount of Transfiguration. You may not always realize this. You may think that the uplifting was just a passing exaltation, but it stamps itself upon your soul and body and marks the planting of a new idea in the upward trend of the whole man. . . .

Having once seen Truth, having once had the illumina-tion, you find that the next step is to demonstrate it and not to be cast down or discouraged by the opposite. When the crucifixion comes and you are suffering the pangs of dying error, you may cry out, "My God, my God, why hast thou forsaken me?" forgetting for the time the promises in the mount of Transfiguration. This is when you need to realize that you are passing through a transforming process that will be followed by a resurrection of all that is worth saving (ASP 150, 152, 155).

When Jesus and His companions joined the nine apostles who had waited at the foot of the mountain, they found them surrounded by a crowd of anxious people. A man from a nearby village had brought his afflicted son to be healed. When he learned that Jesus was away, he asked the apostles for help. They were unable to help, and when Jesus appeared, the father asked Him to heal the child. Jesus said:

Bring him [the child] unto me. And they brought him unto him: and when he saw him, straightway the spirit tare him grievously; and he fell on the ground, and wallowed foaming. And he asked his father, How long time is it since this hath come unto him? And he said, From a child . . . but if thou canst do anything, have compassion on us, and help us. And Jesus said unto him, If thou canst! All things are possible to him that believeth. Straightway the father of the child cried out, and said, I believe; help thou mine unbelief. And when Jesus saw that a multitude came running together, he rebuked the unclean spirit, saying unto him, Thou dumb and deaf spirit, I command thee, come out of him, and enter no more into him. And having cried out, and torn him much, he came out: and *the* boy became as one dead; insomuch that the more part said, He is dead. But Jesus took him by the hand, and raised him up; and he arose (Mark 9:19-27).

Jesus made it plain that the father's faith was necessary for the healing of this affliction of long duration. "All things are possible to him that believeth." Through faith we open ourselves to the healing currents of life that await our acceptance but which cannot be utilized unless we believe. The father did believe in spiritual healing, for he brought his son to Jesus; yet, he knew that his faith was wavering. His heartfelt cry, "I believe; help thou mine unbelief," was the reaching out for a greater faith and the unshakable assurance that Spirit is all-powerful and ever ready to supply man's needs.

The apostles who had been unable to heal the child were puzzled and dismayed at their lack of power. Had they not gone forth "two by two" and done great works in His name? When they were alone with Jesus they asked Him for an explanation of their failure in this instance. His reply was, "This kind can come forth by nothing, but by prayer and fasting" (Mark 9:29 A.V.). Prayer is a positive taking on of spiritual ideas from the Christ Mind; fasting in a spiritual sense is refraining from destructive thought. Jesus' explanation answers the question that comes to those of us who think that we have sufficient faith and who want to do the healing works of the Lord, but often fail. This statement tells us that we have not yet given enough time to prayer or to denial and affirmation. The faithful practice of denial repudiates the error thoughts in consciousness. The consistent practice of affirmations steadies the mind so that the power of God can move through us to heal even deep-rooted mental and physical ailments.

Jesus' return to Capernaum was designedly secret. He did not intend to teach the multitudes again, for He desired to give His time to the training of the Twelve. However, when they reached the city, messengers from the Temple in Jerusalem, whose duty it was to collect the annual Temple tax, saw Peter and asked him if his Master would pay the tax. It was the custom for every Jew over twenty years of age living in Palestine or in foreign countries to pay a tax of half a shekel for the ransom of his soul unto the Lord, and also for the maintenance of the Temple in the Holy City. The tax produced vast sums of money that were conveyed to Jerusalem by messengers who were appointed by the Sanhedrin. Peter was accustomed to paying the tax and perhaps almost subconsciously answered for Jesus also. Then he went to Jesus to get the money.

Jesus may have been amused that He was asked to pay a tax for the ransom of His soul, and He teased Peter some by saying, "What thinkest thou, Simon? the kings of the earth, from whom do they receive toll or tribute? from their sons, or from strangers?" (Matt. 17:25). The answer was obvious, and Peter replied, "From strangers." Jesus pointed out, "Therefore the sons are free."

Peter had no rejoinder. Surely, the Father's son, whom Peter believed Jesus to be, should not have to pay a tax that was paid by sinners! This is one of the occasions on which we get a glimpse of the human side of Jesus and His cordial relationship with His apostles. He knew that He had Peter in a corner, as it were, but He would not desert His friend in his hour of need. Jesus then said:

Go thou to the sea, and cast a hook, and take up the fish that first cometh up; and when thou hast opened his mouth, thou shalt find a shekel: that take, and give unto them for me and thee (Matt. 17:27).

This miracle emphasizes the fact that divine substance is at hand to meet all needs. When we are in tune with the Christ we always know just what to do in order to bring needed substance into visibility. Gold in the fish's mouth tells us that plenty exists in the most unexpected places. We should never limit supply to channels that we know of, but should keep our consciousness receptive to the idea of abundance in order that good can manifest in any of God's ways.

In the days that followed, Jesus often spoke of His impending death and resurrection. It is significant that He never spoke of death without resurrection. We are inclined to speak of death as a finality. When the consciousness is truly one with God, death is a prelude to resurrection. The apostles failed to comprehend Jesus' meaning and discussed among themselves their relative positions in His coming kingdom. They finally asked Him the direct question, "Who then is greatest in the kingdom of heaven?" (Matt. 18:1).

And he called to him a little child, and set him in the midst of them, and said, Verily I say unto you, Except ye turn, and become as little children, ye shall in no wise enter into the kingdom of heaven. Whosoever therefore shall humble himself as this little child, the same is the greatest in the kingdom of heaven. And whoso shall receive one such little child in my name receiveth me (Matt. 18:2-5).

What a lesson in humility this is! The kingdom is not for persons who strive to outdo others; it is for those who have the simplicity, eagerness, and faith of a child. We are children as far as spiritual understanding is concerned. Unless we are humble, reverent toward God, and willing to listen and obey, we cannot receive the gifts He has for us.

As Jesus was talking with them the apostle John, who revealed his ignorance of Jesus' compassion for all men, said:

Teacher, we saw one casting out demons in thy name; and we forbade him, because he followed not us. But Jesus said, Forbid him not: for there is no man who shall do a mighty work in my name, and be able quickly to speak evil of me. For he that is not against us is for us. For whosoever shall give you a cup of water to drink, because ye are Christ's, verily I say unto you, he shall in no wise lose his reward (Mark 9:38-41).

We should recognize and commend good done by others, even though they do not share our beliefs. All good is of God. What difference does it make who does it or what he believes? Persons who do the works of the Father are really one in spirit.

Then came Peter and said to him, Lord, how oft shall my brother sin against me, and I forgive him? until seven times? Jesus saith unto him, I say not unto thee, Until seven times; but, Until seventy times seven (Matt. 18:21, 22).

And He told them the parable of the unmerciful servant (Matt. 18:23-35). It teaches the lesson that when we cannot do as we should, that is, cannot fulfill the obligations that are rightly expected of us, we quickly ask forgiveness and receive it. But how do we treat persons who fail to fulfill their obligations to us? Are we harsh and unforgiving? If so, our own deficiencies cannot be overlooked. When it seems that people harm us, it is only because we are looking at situations with our material eyes. Our good is always secure, for it is in God, who is ever with us. When, therefore, we appear to be wronged by others (our brother sins against us), we are to forgive "seventy times seven," or an unlimited number of times.

We must forgive as we would be forgiven. To forgive does not simply mean to arrive at a place of indifference to those who do personal injury to us; it means far more than this. To forgive is to give for—to give some actual, definite good in return for evil given. . . .

The very pain that you suffer, the very failure to demonstrate over some matter that touches your own life deeply, may rest upon just this spirit of unforgiveness that you harbor toward the world in general. Put it away with resolution *(Lessons in Truth* 14).

CHAPTER IX

Later Judean Ministry

(Third Year)

IT WAS AUTUMN, and many Galileans were preparing to go to the Feast of Tabernacles in Jerusalem. On the eve of their departure to attend this feast, "His brethren" urged Jesus to go to Judea. Though these brethren did not believe in Him, He was an outstanding figure, and they could not understand why He kept Himself in obscurity. "Manifest thyself to the world," they said (John 7:4). Jesus refused, "My time is not yet come" (John 7:6). However, after they had left, Jesus did go to Jerusalem, "not publicly, but as it were in secret" (John 7:10). He knew the trip would be a dangerous one for Him and, probably, He did not want to involve others in what might occur.

The trip led through Samaria, and Jesus sent the apostles James and John to make arrangements for lodging in a village. The Samaritans refused to receive Him because He was on His way to Jerusalem, and the haughty bearing of the Jerusalem Jews had caused the Samaritans to hate them. The Samaritans' lack of hospitality so angered the two apostles that they said, "Lord, wilt thou that we command fire to come down from heaven, and consume them?" (Luke 9:54). But Jesus rebuked them, and they went on to another village (Luke 9:54).

James represents the quality of judgment; John

represents the quality of love, and both of them acted
in a very unspiritual fashion in this instance. Until
our twelve spiritual faculties, represented by the
apostles, have been redeemed they ofttimes go awry,
even though we are walking in the Way as well as
we can. It is almost encouraging to see in this instance a limited expression of our inherent powers
of judgment and love (James and John), because
they often have a limited expression in us! When
our judgment wants to condemn and our love
temporarily leaves and is replaced by a desire to
destroy, we need not be discouraged. Instead, we
should listen and learn from the great Teacher.

The thousands of Jews who flocked to Jerusalem
for the Feast of Tabernacles were eager to see Him.
"Where is he?" (John 7:11) they asked. In the
midst of the celebrations Jesus appeared in the
Temple and began teaching the people. They marveled at what He said, and asked, "How knoweth
this man letters, never having learned?" (John
7:15). Jesus had not attended the rabbinical schools
in Jerusalem; yet, He spoke with wisdom and authority that far surpassed that of the great scholars:

My teaching is not mine, but his that sent me. If any
man willeth to do his will, he shall know of the teaching,
whether it is of God, or *whether* I speak from myself. He
that speaketh from himself seeketh his own glory: but
he that seeketh the glory of him that sent him, the same is
true, and no unrighteousness is in him (John 7:16-18).

The all-knowing Christ Mind in us will teach us

when we are willing to listen, but we must lay aside our own beliefs if we would learn from our Father.

Jesus went on to say that in one sense the Jews knew the law which Moses had given them; yet, in another sense they were pitiably ignorant of it. Then He asked them bluntly, "Why seek ye to kill me?" (John 7:19). He knew that the Jewish leaders had sent men to take Him, but the people generally were unaware of this and asked who was threatening His life. Without answering, Jesus reminded them that in accordance with the Mosaic Law a man could be circumcised on the Sabbath; but that they were angry when He healed a man on the Sabbath. He admonished them, "Judge not according to appearance, but judge righteous judgment" (John 7:24).

This verse on judgment has an exceedingly important teaching that we should remember. Any appearance of limitation is deceptive, for God is omnipresent. It is wise to look for reality beyond every negative appearance, and spiritual perception makes it possible for us to do this. We may see divine order that is beyond the display of disorder, love that is beyond the show of hate, and wholeness that is beyond the manifestation of disease. To behold the good that exists in the very midst of any appearance of evil is indeed to "judge righteous judgment."

On the last and great day of the feast, Jesus again attempted to convince His countrymen that His was a divine mission.

If any man thirst, let him come unto me and drink. He

that believeth on me, as the scripture hath said, from within him shall flow rivers of living water. But this spake he of the Spirit, which they that believed on him were to receive (John 7:37-39).

After His declaration some said that Jesus was a prophet, and others accepted Him as the Christ. But some wondered how the Christ could be a Galilean, when the Scriptures said that He would be of the seed of David and would come from the city of Bethlehem. "So there arose a division in the multitude because of him. And some of them would have taken him; but no man laid hands on him" (John 7:43, 44).

Up to this time only the Pharisees had opposed Jesus, but now the Sadducees, the second most important party among the Jews, joined with them in active hostility toward Him. Though they were smaller in number than the Pharisaic party, the Sadducees were the aristocracy. They openly courted the favor of the Romans and had been rewarded with great political power. The Pharisees' enmity for Jesus came from the fear that He would destroy their sacred law, but the Sadducees, who were far more material in their interests, paid scant attention to Him until it was evident that He was gaining much influence over the masses. At last, considering Him a religious fanatic, the Sadducees decided that it would be better to have Him out of the way, for He might stir up trouble in Palestine and jeopardize their prestige and authority. Therefore, the Sadducees acted with the Pharisees and sent officers from the Sanhedrin, the supreme court of the Jews, to bring Jesus before this court for trial.

The Sanhedrin, located in Jerusalem, was composed of seventy-one members selected from prominent Sadducees and Pharisees. The high priest was appointed by the Roman government and was invariably a Sadducee. The court had jurisdiction over religious and civil matters affecting Jews, but it lacked authority to pass the death sentence.

When the officers failed to take Jesus captive, they were summoned before the Sanhedrin in order that they might explain. "Never man so spake" (John 7:47), they declared, in excusing themselves. The members of the court chided them for being "led astray," and pointed out that they, the Jewish leaders, considered Him a false prophet. Only one voice in the Sanhedrin was raised in Jesus' defense: that of Nicodemus. He reminded them that the Jewish law did not condemn a man without giving him a chance to defend himself. Sneeringly they asked, "Art thou of Galilee?" (John 7:52), implying that Nicodemus was a follower of the Nazarene.

The next day Jesus returned to the Temple, where He was called on to use the wisdom and compassion of Christ in dealing with a woman taken in adultery. She was brought to Him by the scribes and Pharisees, who wanted to trick Jesus into taking a stand that would discredit Him with the people. The Law of Moses prescribed death by stoning for an adulteress, but this punishment had been abandoned long before, since the Jews had become indifferent in upholding the moral code. Then, too, Judea was a Roman province and only the Roman procurator could pronounce the death verdict. However, if Jesus failed to uphold the Mosaic Law, the people would not consider Him a prophet. If He did uphold it, He would show himself pitiless, and, in addition, would break the Roman law.

But Jesus stooped down, and with his finger wrote on the ground. But when they continued asking him, he lifted up himself, and said unto them, He that is without sin among you, let him first cast a stone at her. . . . And they, when they heard it, went out one by one, beginning from the eldest, *even* unto the last: and Jesus was left alone, and the woman, where she was, in the midst. And Jesus lifted up himself, and said unto her, Woman, where are they? did no man condemn thee? And she said, No man, Lord. And Jesus said, Neither do I condemn thee: go thy way; from henceforth sin no more (John 8:6-11).

Jesus never condoned vice of any kind.

His wisdom in handling this case teaches us that there is always a way to work out complex situations in line with Principle. "Sin no more," He said; yet He was compassionate of sinners. He knew that the persons who condemned the woman were guilty of many evils and He gave them opportunity to see themselves in their true light. At the same time, He gave the woman opportunity to live a better life in the future. Sometimes it seems that we must choose between a cruel act and upholding wrongdoing. Only the Christ can tell us how to act in accordance with Principle, and when we do everyone is benefited.

During the Feast of Tabernacles the people, the priests, and the Pharisees joined in festal dances to the music of flutes and other instruments. The Levites stood on the fifteen steps leading to the court and chanted the majestic Psalms known as the Songs of Ascent (Psalms 120-134). Lighted by gigantic candelabra some fifty cubits in height and splendidly gilded, the scene was a very impressive one. Undoubtedly, the memory of its splendor lingered long in the minds of all who witnessed it.

In this setting, Jesus later gave the teaching in which He referred to Himself as the light of the world:

I am the light of the world: he that followeth me shall not walk in the darkness, but shall have the light of life (John 8:12).

The Pharisees immediately took exception to His words. The spiritually illumined mind, which Jesus represents, and the limited human mind, represented by the Jewish leaders, are in sharp conflict. They speak a different language, and neither can understand the other. The things of the Spirit must be spiritually discerned, and so long as a person is in the Pharisaic state of consciousness he is not able to see beyond the literal interpretation of religion. Thus, the Christ word is incomprehensible. Jesus said to them:

Ye are from beneath: I am from above: ye are of this world; I am not of this world. . . . for except ye believe that I am *he,* ye shall die in your sins. . . . When ye have lifted up the Son of man, then shall ye know that I am *he,* and *that* I do nothing of myself, but as the Father taught me, I speak these things (John 8:23-27).

It is only when our consciousness is raised to the higher realm (the Son of man is lifted up) that we recognize and understand the word of one who speaks from the Christ level.

As Jesus spoke, "many believed on him." To them He said,

If ye abide in my word, *then* are ye truly my disciples; and ye shall know the truth, and the truth shall make you free (John 8:31-32).

Man is a son of God and has within him the divine life of his Father. Unless we hold to this true view and obey the promptings of Spirit within, we cannot gain real freedom.

But the Jews insisted that they were already free. They claimed that they were "Abraham's seed" and, therefore, were not in bondage to any man.

Verily, verily, I say unto you, Every one that committeth sin is the bondservant of sin. And the bondservant abideth not in the house for ever: the son abideth for ever. If therefore the Son shall make you free, ye shall be free indeed (John 8:34-36).

Charles Fillmore states:

The "house" is man's body. No one who allows intemperate desires to rule his life and to gain expression

through his thought and conduct can hope to remain long
in the body or to experience in it any measure of true satisfaction. Only the "son," the self-forgetting, loving, helpful concentration of all the powers upon the gaining of a
higher understanding of the forces that control mankind,
can bring full and complete freedom. Once this power of
concentration is gained and practiced, perfect freedom is
indeed assured. But concentration does not spring, perfect
and full-fledged, from beneath the fleeting wing of the
random resolve; it requires the faithful giving of oneself
to the practice of the presence of God. "Abideth" entails a
continuing in the Christ state of mind and heart (MJ 88).

Surely "Abraham's children" would be righteous, they insisted, thus showing their dependence
on human ancestry. Jesus reminded them that if they
were Abraham's children in the true sense of the
word, they would do his works. Instead, the Jews
sought to kill Jesus, who taught Truth as He received
it from God. "If God were your Father, ye would
love me: for I came forth and am come from God"
(John 8:42). "Verily, verily I say unto you, if a man
keep my word, he shall never see death" (John 8:51).

The words of Jesus were more powerful than
those of any other man, but here the word as used
means the creative Word of God, the Logos. Jesus
"infused the divine-life idea into His words until
they made direct union with the creative Word of
the Father" (MJ 93).

Charles Fillmore goes on to say:

When man in faith makes this intimate connection between his mind and the Father's, he enters into what may

be termed the "river of life," and he has ability to take others with him into the waters that cleanse, purify, and vitalize so perfectly that death is swallowed up in life and man lives right on without the tragedy of death. Such a man was, and is, Jesus the Christ, and the promise is that all who incorporate in mind and body the living creative Word, as He did, will with Him escape death. This promise of the overcoming power of the Word has been interpreted to mean death of the soul after physical death, but there is no foundation for this assumption. Jesus overcame death of the body. His followers are expected to do the same (MJ 93).

To the Jews, Jesus' statement was quite unreasonable. They knew that Abraham and the prophets were dead. "Whom makest thou thyself?" they demanded.

Jesus answered, If I glorify myself my glory is nothing: it is my Father that glorifieth me; of whom ye say, that he is your God; and ye have not known him . . . but I know him, and keep his word. Your father Abraham rejoiced to see my day (John 8:54-56).

The Jews reminded Jesus that He was not yet fifty years of age, and they refused to believe that He had seen Abraham. Jesus replied, "Verily, verily, I say unto you, Before Abraham was born, I am" (John 8:58).

Jesus was speaking from the plane of the Christ, the everlasting self of man, without beginning and without end. The Christ had existed before man came into being and will exist throughout the eons of time. He is spiritual man, created in God's image and likeness. Jesus knew Himself to be one with Christ, and He declared His eternal livingness.

The Jews were so angered by Jesus' statement that they picked up stones to throw at Him, but He hid Himself and went out of the Temple.

And as he passed by, he saw a man blind from his birth. And his disciples asked him, saying, Rabbi, who sinned, this man, or his parents, that he should be born blind? Jesus answered, Neither did this man sin, nor his parents: but that the works of God should be made manifest in him. We must work the works of him that sent me, while it is day: the night cometh, when no man can work. When I am in the world, I am the light of the world. When he had thus spoken, he spat on the ground, and made clay of the spittle, and anointed his eyes with the clay, and said unto him, Go, wash in the pool of Siloam (which is by interpretation, Sent). He went away therefore, and washed, and came seeing (John 9:1-7).

When the people saw the man who had been healed of blindness, they were amazed, and asked him who had restored his sight. When he replied that he did not know, he was taken to the Pharisees to whom he told his story. It was the Sabbath, and some of the Pharisees said, "This man [the healer] is not from God, because he keepeth not the sabbath" (John 9:16). But several asked how a sinner could do such marvelous works, and some suggested that perhaps the man had not really been blind from birth. So they sought out his parents and questioned them. His parents testified that their son had been born blind, but they knew nothing of how his healing had come about. "Ask him; he is of age." This the Pharisees did, and tried to make him retract his story. They insisted that only God could heal, and that surely a sinner could not have opened his eyes. The man's firm response was: "Whether he is a sinner, I know not: one thing I know, that, whereas I was blind, now I see" (John 9:25). The Jews then became so angry that they cast the man out of the Temple.

The apostles' question, "Who sinned, this man, or his parents that he should be born blind?" reveals the Jewish belief that distress of body or circumstances was the direct result of disobedience to God's law—sin. Was the man's blindness caused by his own sin? This blindness did not result from a sin that was committed during his life, for he had been blind at birth. The question shows the general acceptance of reincarnation among the Jews, which holds that the sins of a former life are outpictured as difficulties in a person's present existence. However, as the man had not overcome the condition growing out of the failures of a previous life, he was guilty of what Charles Fillmore calls a "sin of omission":

Before he was healed, the blind man was a sinner of omission. He was a blind beggar, a person who had no perception of his own capacity, or no confidence in his powers to rise superior to conditions in the material realm. When man fails to apprehend his mission and to do the work of bringing forth the good that is allotted to him, he remains in darkness. His blindness is that sin of omission which is present in every man who does not realize his place in the Godhead. If a man fails to do that which he is told from within is the right thing to do, he is sinning, and his soul will remain in darkness to just the degree that he sins (MJ 97).

The second part of the question asks if the sins of the man's parents were responsible for his affliction. To this day many persons believe in inherited weaknesses. Jesus refuted this also. He saw in the condition an opportunity to bring forth the wholeness that God ordained for man ("the works of God should be made manifest in him"). When we are in bondage to some form of limitation, be it physical or mental, it does little good to argue as to who was at fault. Is it not far better to have faith that the healing can and will come through?

The works of God that we are to make manifest are the perfect ideas of a perfect-man idea in Divine Mind. "Ye therefore shall be perfect, as your heavenly Father is perfect." We are to bring forth in ourselves the perfection of Being. If through neglect, laziness, or belief in inability we fail to do this, we fall under the judgment of the constantly operating law of life, which is inwardly urging us, and in all the visible and invisible forms of nature is commanding, "Go forward."

The world is full of people who are in this beggarly blind state. They sit by the wayside and wait for the workers to give them pennies and crusts, when they themselves might be the producers of their own good. The remedy for this situation is for them to deny material darkness, ignorance, and inability in themselves. By putting the clay upon the blind man's eyes Jesus illustrated how man makes opaque his understanding by affirming the power of material conditions to hamper and impede his spiritual and material growth. The washing away of this clay by the man himself shows that by our own volition and our own efforts we must deny away these seeming mountains of environing conditions (MJ 97, 98).

Hearing that the Pharisees had driven the man from the Temple, Jesus located him, and the man affirmed his faith in Jesus as the Son of God. When we take our stand with Christ, the Pharisees in our mental realm oppose us and try to convince us that we are doing something wrong (put us out of the Temple). If, however, we hold to our spiritual conviction, we shall continue to see clearly and shall worship God in spirit and in Truth. The mortal thoughts are blind, and Jesus took this occasion to give the Pharisees a lesson on true and false teachers:

Verily, verily, I say unto you, He that entereth not by the door into the fold of the sheep, but climbeth up by some other way, the same is a thief and a robber. But he that entereth in by the door is the shepherd of the sheep. To him the porter openeth; and the sheep hear his voice: and he calleth his own sheep by name, and leadeth them out. When he hath put forth all his own, he goeth before them, and the sheep follow him; for they know his voice. And a stranger will they not follow, but will flee from him: for they know not the voice of strangers (John 10:1-15).

The I AM (Christ) is the good shepherd who tenderly cares for His sheep (thoughts). The thoughts that enter our minds "some other way" than by the door (spiritual inspiration) are thieves and robbers (error thoughts). Christ's sheep (spiritual ideas) know the voice of the shepherd (I AM) and follow Him. When strangers (error thoughts) come and would destroy them, the sheep do not hear them. "I am the good shepherd: the good shepherd layeth down his life for the sheep" (John 10:11).

This means that the high spiritual I AM lets itself become identified with the limitations of self-consciousness that it may lift all up to the spiritual plane. "I lay down my life, that I may take it again."

When we open the door of the mind by consciously affirming the presence and power of the divine I AM in our midst, there is a marriage or union of the higher forces in being with the lower, and we find that we are quickened in every part; the life of the I AM has been poured out for us. Thus Christ becomes the Saviour of the whole world by pouring this higher spiritual energy (His blood) into human consciousness, which each must take for himself and identify himself with. The individual I AM is the only door through which it can get into our thoughts in a legitimate way. If it comes through mediumship or hypnotism or mental suggestion, without our willing co-operation, it is "a thief and a robber" (MJ 101, 102).

When Jesus concluded,

There arose a division again among the Jews because of these words. And many of them said, He hath a demon, and is mad; why hear ye him? Others said, These are not the sayings of one possessed with a demon. Can a demon open the eyes of the blind? (John 10:19-21).

The differences of opinion among the Jews about Jesus signify the uncertainty of the mind in its human intellectual state. It argues back and forth, swinging from belief in Christ to rejection of Him.

Jesus realized that nothing further could be accomplished in Jerusalem, and He returned to Galilee for a brief stay. A short time later, He appointed seventy disciples to go on a missionary tour. The word *disciple* is often used to designate persons who believed in Jesus and accepted His teaching. They were His general followers. The word *apostle* is applied to the twelve men whom Jesus called and who accompanied Him during the three years of His ministry. Jesus "sent them [the seventy disciples] two and two before his face into every city and place, whither he himself was about to come" (Luke 10:1).

Jesus' instructions to the Seventy were similar to those He gave to the Twelve (see *Chapter VII*). When they returned, probably several weeks later, they were exceedingly joyous, and said:

Lord, even the demons are subject unto us in thy name. And he said unto them, I beheld Satan fallen as lightning from heaven. Behold, I have given you authority to tread upon serpents and scorpions, and over all the power of the enemy: and nothing shall in any wise hurt you. Nevertheless in this rejoice not, that the spirits are subject unto you; but rejoice that your names are written in heaven (Luke 10:17-20).

When we go forth "in His name" and feel spiritual power operating through us, we are happy and grateful. Jesus' remark that He "beheld Satan fallen as lightning from heaven" means that error thoughts (Satan), which have invaded the harmony of mind (heaven), are dislodged by the spiritual word. By holding fast to Truth we have power over conditions that would ordinarily injure us (serpents, scorpions, and the enemy). Jesus warns, however, that we are not to rejoice in the outer demonstration itself but, rather, to rejoice that we have attained a greater degree of spiritual awareness and authority (our names are written in heaven).

The last six months of Jesus' ministry were to mark an increasing hostility on the part of Jewish leaders and a more stern mood on His part. He traveled rapidly from place to place, going several times into Judea. On one of these brief visits, a scribe (called a lawyer in the Bible text), thinking to confuse Jesus, asked:

> Teacher, what shall I do to inherit eternal life? And he said unto him, What is written in the law? how readest thou? And he answering said, Thou shalt love the Lord thy God with all thy heart, and with all thy soul, and with all thy strength, and with all thy mind; and thy neighbor as thyself. And he said unto him, Thou hast answered right: this do, and thou shalt live. But he, desiring to justify himself, said unto Jesus, And who is my neighbor? (Luke 10:25-29).

In answer to this question, Jesus gave one of the most beautiful of the parables, the parable of the Good Samaritan (Luke 10:30-37). Our neighbor is anyone who is nearby and needs assistance, whether he be friend or stranger. We cannot expect to correct all the ills of the world but we can help the people with whom we come in contact. This is our spiritual service. Sometimes this need is satisfied by a kind or inspiring word, sometimes physical aid is necessary. Often our most effective service is to pray for others. It is not by chance that certain people come into the orbit of our lives. They are drawn to us by the law of attraction, and we should not, like the priest and the Levite, pass by "on the other side." According to the Jews, a Samaritan was inferior racially and religiously, but he was more truly spiritual than those of whom righteousness was expected. Jesus Himself was playing the part of the Good Samaritan by telling this parable to a Jewish scribe who, bound by the letter of the law, could easily overlook its spirit.

Finally Jesus reached Bethany, a small village a few miles to the south of Jerusalem. In this village lived His three friends, Martha, Mary, and their brother Lazarus. The three comprised a family in easy circumstances, and of sufficient dignity and position to excite considerable attention in their own village and even in Jerusalem, as was proved later when Lazarus was raised from the dead. Martha welcomed Jesus and began to prepare a feast for her renowned guest, Mary "sat at the Lord's feet, and heard his word" (Luke 10:39).

But Martha was cumbered about much serving; and she came up to him, and said, Lord, dost thou not care that my sister did leave me to serve alone? bid her therefore that she help me. But the Lord answered and said unto her, Martha, Martha, thou art anxious and troubled about many things: but one thing is needful: for Mary hath chosen the good part, which shall not be taken away from her (Luke 10:40-42).

Women represent the emotional or feeling nature, and the two sisters symbolize love operating on different levels. Martha's love was expressed by ministering to the physical needs of Jesus, whereas Mary's love bade her listen to His words. It is good to serve in an outer way, but it is better still to take time to sit at the Lord's feet and give attention to what He says (study and pray). Jesus commended Mary, for she had chosen the higher office of love, which is worship. "But one thing is needful," He said. That one thing is what we should have above all else, even to this day—a devotion to Christ and a willingness to devote some time to the contemplation of that which is divine.

And it came to pass, as he was praying in a certain place, that when he ceased, one of his disciples said unto him, Lord, teach us to pray, even as John also taught his disciples (Luke 11:1).

The verses that follow in the Gospel of Luke record a shorter form of the Lord's Prayer than the one given in the Sermon on the Mount (Matt. 6:9-13). Jesus expanded His teaching on prayer by giving the parable of the importunate friend (Luke 11:5-8). This parable emphasizes the necessity of persistence in prayer. Our Father is not reluctant to answer our requests, but we often have to ask Him a number of times in order to develop the faith that will enable us to receive. Jesus gave the assurance of answered prayer in the words:

Ask, and it shall be given you; seek, and ye shall find; knock, and it shall be opened unto you. For every one that asketh receiveth; and he that seeketh findeth; and to him that knocketh it shall be opened" (Luke 11:9, 10).

Then Jesus showed the similarity between the love of our heavenly Father and that of an earthly father. If the earthly father loves his children and wants to give them good gifts, "how much more shall *your* heavenly Father give the Holy Spirit to them that ask him?" (Luke 11:13).

While Jesus was still in Judea, He again denounced the scribes and Pharisees, "for ye tithe mint and rue and every herb, and pass over justice and the love of God: but these ought ye to have done, and not to leave the other undone" (Luke 11:42). As Jesus was speaking, a crowd gathered about Him. However, He addressed Himself to the Twelve, warning them to beware of the "leaven of the Pharisees, which is hypocrisy" (Luke 12:1). Hidden sins will come to light. Jesus said, "There is nothing covered up, that shall not be revealed; and hid, that shall not be known" (Luke 12:2, 3). Whatever abides in our consciousness must manifest itself eventually. We cannot prevent destructive thoughts from outpicturing in our bodies and circumstances.

A person in the crowd asked Jesus to compel his brother to divide an inheritance with him. Jesus refused and said, "Take heed, and keep yourselves from all covetousness: for a man's life consisteth not in the abundance of the things which he possesseth" (Luke 12:15). To illustrate His point, Jesus gave the parable of the rich fool (Luke 12:16-21). The person who lays up treasures for himself and neglects his spiritual obligations is shortsighted and foolish. When men leave the body they cannot take material possessions with them, but they are compelled to take the consciousness that they have acquired. If we have given time and thought to gaining spiritual treasures—understanding, love, and peace—we are "rich toward God," and He will see that we lack no good thing. "Fear not, little flock; for it is your Father's good pleasure to give you the kingdom" (Luke 12:32).

Jesus followed this teaching with another parable, the parable of the waiting servants (Luke 12: 35-40). It brings out the lesson that we should keep our consciousness so constructive ("let your loins be girded about, and your lamps burning") that we will be ready for a spiritual realization (our Lord) at any time, "for in an hour that ye think not, the Son of man cometh."

In further explanation of the preceding parable, Jesus told the parable of the wise steward (Luke 12:41-48). We are stewards, appointed by our Lord to do His work in the world. When we are faithful in the performance of our tasks, the Father gives us authority and dominion ("he will set him over all that he hath"). If, on the other hand, we disregard His commandments and foolishly think that there will not be a day of reckoning, "the lord of that servant shall come in a day when he expecteth not . . . and shall cut him asunder, and appoint his portion with the unfaithful." The lord represents the law of cause and effect, always operative and rendering to each person his just deserts. When we understand God's requirements and fail to fulfill them, our punishment from the law is severe, for "to whomsoever much is given, of him shall much be required."

About this time word was brought to Jesus that a resistance movement against the Roman government had been detected by Pontius Pilate, and a number of Galileans had been slain. Jesus gave the group a warning against wrongdoing of any kind. He intimated that the Galileans who had perished because they revolted against Rome were no more sinful than other men, even those dwelling in Jerusalem who prated of their piety. "I tell you, Nay: but, except ye repent, ye shall all in like manner perish" (Luke 13:3).

The parable of the barren fig tree (Luke 13:6-9) illustrates His point. Unless we practice the principles of right thinking and acting, we are like a fig tree that bears no fruit. Our failure to produce spiritually separates us from our Lord, and we are worthless ("Why doth it also cumber the ground?"). Jesus, whose mission was to save mankind, is likened to the vinedresser who pleaded with the owner of the vineyard to spare the tree for a time that he might give it special care in the hope that it would bring forth figs. It seemed that even at this time in His ministry Jesus still hoped that the Jews would accept Him and rectify their lives. This parable brings to mind the consoling fact that even though we may have failed to put our spiritual resources to good use, our Father is still patient and gives us another chance.

As Jesus traveled about the country He often taught in a synagogue on the Sabbath.

Behold, a woman that had a spirit of infirmity eighteen years; and she was bowed together, and could in no wise lift herself up. And when Jesus saw her, he called her, and said to her, Woman, thou art loosed from thine infirmity. And he laid his hands upon her: and immediately she was made straight, and glorified God (Luke 13:11-13).

This healing is unusual in that the woman did not ask for it. It brings out the thought that when we turn to God (symbolized by the woman's attending a religious service), we can be benefited in ways we do not foresee. The lifted consciousness is what makes us receptive to divine blessings; and by seeking God we invariably find some portion of His good.

CHAPTER X

Perean Ministry

(Third Year)

THERE WAS great rejoicing in Jerusalem, for it was again time for the Feast of the Dedication. This feast, held each winter, and lasting eight days, commemorated the cleansing of the Temple by Judas Maccabeus in 165 B.C., after it had been profaned by the King of Syria.

The eastern porch of the Temple was called Solomon's Porch, because it was built of material that had been preserved from the original Temple. Here Jesus was walking on the porch when He was surrounded by a group of Jews who asked:

How long dost thou hold us in suspense? If thou art the Christ, tell us plainly. Jesus answered them, I told you, and ye believe not: the works that I do in my Father's name, these bear witness of me (John 10:24, 25).

"By their fruits ye shall know them," was the substance of Jesus' words. He had done great works that could be done only by one who knew "I and the Father are one" (John 10:30). However, to the Jewish leaders His words were blasphemous, and again they took up stones to slay Him:

Jesus answered them, Many good works have I showed you from the Father; for which of those works do ye stone me? The Jews answered him, For a good work we stone thee not, but for blasphemy; and because that thou, being a man, makest thyself God (John 10:32, 33).

Jesus reminded them that their Scriptures said, "Ye are gods" (Psalms 82:6). Why, then, did they refuse to believe Him when He claimed to be divine? "If I do not the works of my Father, believe me not. But if I do them, though ye believe not me, believe the works: that ye may know and understand that the Father is in me, and I in the Father" (John 10:37, 38).

Spiritual works are the natural expression of one established in the realization of oneness with Christ. But those persons who consider themselves religious and yet cannot heal or perform so-called miracles are at a loss to understand the person who can. In their ignorance they bitterly oppose him and seek to belittle what he does.

The Jews tried again to take Jesus, but they could not. Perhaps something of the majesty of His being deterred them. After the Feast of Dedication "he went forth out of their hand" (John 10:39), retiring to the section of Palestine known as Perea, east of the Jordan and across the river from Judea.

It was now only three or four months until the Passover, at which time Jesus was to be crucified. During these months Jesus traveled from place to place, going into Judea on several occasions. His days were filled with teaching and good works. Contests with His enemies were sharper, and the conditions He imposed for discipleship were more stringent. Much of His instruction was presented through parables, thirteen of which were given in these last few months. The raising of Lazarus was the outstanding event in this period, and Jesus' lifted consciousness, which was evident at this time, was a fitting prelude to His resurrection.

As Jesus went through a Perean village He was asked, "Lord, are they few that be saved?" (Luke 13:23). "Strive to enter in by the narrow door: for many . . . shall seek to enter in, and shall not be able," was His answer (Luke 13:24). The narrow door signifies that those who wish to "enter in" must strictly adhere to spiritual principle; otherwise, they will be shut out, and "There shall be the weeping and the gnashing of teeth, when ye shall see Abraham and Isaac, and Jacob, and all the prophets, in the kingdom of God, and yourselves cast forth without" (Luke 13:28). There is nothing harsh or unjust about this adherence. The law of God that governs our lives is exact, and unless we comply with this law we cannot expect to receive its rich benefits.

Wherever Jesus went, the Pharisees kept a watchful eye on Him. One Sabbath a ruler of the Pharisees invited Him to dinner. The critical attitude of the guests caused Jesus to tell the parable of the guests at feasts (Luke 14:7-11), a lesson in true humility. Jesus explained that the most important guest at a banquet should have the seat of honor next to the host (chief seat), but instead of waiting to be invited, the Jews would often lose all sense of decorum and struggle for the coveted place. Jesus

taught that a person should select the lowest seat
(humble himself), and then wait to be moved higher
(be exalted). He pointed out that a person can easily
lose worldly prestige when he is striving for the
chief place and is then forced to take the lowest
place. The feeling of insecurity and selfishness in
each of us is revealed when we push ourselves forward. Our true worth insures us an honorable place
without any effort on our part. "For every one that
exalteth himself shall be humbled; and he that
humbleth himself shall be exalted" (Luke 14:11).

And he said to him also that had bidden him, When
thou makest a dinner or a supper, call not thy friends, nor
thy brethren, nor thy kinsmen, nor rich neighbors; lest
haply they also bid thee again, and a recompense be made
thee. But when thou makest a feast, bid the poor, the
maimed, the lame, the blind; and thou shalt be blessed;
because they have not *wherewith* to recompense thee; for
thou shalt be recompensed in the resurrection of the just
(Luke 14:12-14).

All of us are not to give with the hope of getting
something in return, but we are to help others who
are less fortunate than ourselves. The law of love
rewards us.

One of the guests at the ruler's dinner remarked
that it was blessed indeed to "eat bread in the kingdom of God," and in answer Jesus told the parable
of the great supper (Luke 14:16-24). From it we
learn that we are all invited to God's feast (an abundance of divine ideas). Do we consent to partake
of it or do we make excuses? The person who is

absorbed in materiality slights the things of Spirit ("I have bought a field, and I must needs go out and see it"). The person who is enslaved by his animal tendencies also turns aside ("I have bought five yoke of oxen, and I go to prove them"). The one who loves personality revels in the joy of it and refuses to give his attention to God ("I have married a wife, and therefore I cannot come"). The persons who are in trouble ("the poor and maimed and blind and lame") are glad to accept the Lord's bounty. The derelicts (those who are found in the "highways and hedges") are compelled to come to the feast. Persons who have reached the lowest level in life can turn to God. In so doing they appropriate divine ideas (eat of the feast) and are nourished, whereas those who make excuses cannot "taste of my supper."

As the multitudes followed Him Jesus cautioned them to count the cost before they decided to become His disciples:

If any man cometh unto me, and hateth not his own father, and mother, and wife, and children, and brethren, and sisters, yea, and his own life also, he cannot be my disciple. Whosoever doth not bear his own cross, and come after me, cannot be my disciple. . . . So therefore whosoever he be of you that renounceth not all that he hath, he cannot be my disciple (Luke 14:26, 27, 33).

These are powerful words, and they have often been misinterpreted. They mean that when we desire to tread the spiritual path we must put God before any human relationships and even before life itself.

By so doing we do not neglect our responsibilities to our families. Rather, we fulfill them more fully because we give prime consideration to our Lord and draw wisdom and love from Him. To bear our cross is to take upon ourselves the task of eliminating the qualities in us that do not measure up to a spiritual ideal. We must carefully consider the price to be paid for spiritual enlightenment and power.

Jesus further illustrated the requirements for discipleship in the parable of the tower and the king. A wise man does not attempt to build a tower without first making sure that he can complete it. Neither would a wise king undertake to conquer an army without first considering whether he had sufficient strength to win the battle. Likewise, if we expect to build spiritual strength (a tower) or overcome adverse thoughts (an army), we must be certain of the firmness of our resolve and of our willingness to co-operate with Spirit in order that Spirit may express through us. In other words, we must put love of God before anything else.

Now all the publicans and sinners were drawing near unto him to hear him. And both the Pharisees and the scribes murmured, saying, This man receiveth sinners, and eateth with them (Luke 15:1, 2).

In rapid succession Jesus gave three parables in defense of His compassion for and interest in sinners. These are the parables of the lost sheep, the lost coin, and the prodigal son.

In the parable of the lost sheep (Luke 15:3-7),

Jesus taught the love of the Christ (owner of the sheep) for His children, good and bad (all the sheep). The lost sheep represents the person who has strayed from the path of righteousness, yet the owner (the Christ) leaves the sheep that are safe in the fold (the ninety and nine) and seeks the one that is lost. When He finds him there is great rejoicing. "I say unto you, that even so there shall be joy in heaven over one sinner that repenteth, *more* than over ninety and nine righteous persons, who need no repentance."

The parable of the lost coin (Luke 15:8-10) expands the idea that every individual is important to Christ. The lost coin symbolizes the erring person who must be diligently sought until recovered. The owner of the coin is the one who searches for it, even as the Christ always seeks to reclaim the lost. There is rejoicing "over one sinner that repenteth."

Perhaps the best known and loved of Jesus' parables is that of the prodigal son (Luke 15:11-32). The younger son symbolizes the person who has not yet been awakened to his spiritual nature and who takes his inheritance (divine substance) from his father (God) and departs into a "far country" (material consciousness). There he squanders his resources of mind and body in sense gratification ("wasted his substance with riotous living"), and the inevitable result is depletion ("want"). Because man is innately spiritual, he gradually awakens to his true nature (the prodigal "came to himself") and realizes that happiness and fulfillment can come only by a reunion with God ("I will arise and go to my father"). The prodigal is aware of his sins, seeks forgiveness, and shows his willingness to return to his father's house and take a lowly position. "Father, I have sinned against heaven, and in thy sight: I am no more worthy to be called thy son: make me as one of thy hired servants." But God is love, and love is extended to the repentant one regardless of his iniquities. "While he was yet afar off, his father saw him, and was moved with compassion, and ran, and fell on his neck, and kissed him." As the prodigal makes contact with the divine source, abundance of good flows forth. His father gives him the best robe, a ring, shoes, and an opulent feast. "For this my son was dead, and is alive again; he was lost, and is found."

The elder brother was unforgiving and harsh in judging his brother, and showed no pleasure in his return. He was jealous of his father's blessing extended to one whom he considered unworthy. He was envious of his brother's good fortune and his reinstatement in the home. He was sullen and angry, and would not attend the feast. Like the Pharisees to whom Jesus told the parable, the elder brother was self-righteous. "Lo, these many years do I serve thee, and I never transgressed a commandment of thine." No one is less merciful than he who is unaware of any fault in himself. Persons who know they have fallen short of goodness and ask forgiveness come into the kingdom more quickly than those whose eyes are closed to their own shortcomings.

Yet the elder brother is also a child of God and is reminded of his right to share in His good, "Son, thou art ever with me, and all that is mine is thine."

Jesus told three parables on stewardship after He had finished the parables that showed His great interest in sinners. The first, the parable of the unjust steward, was given to some disciples; the second, the parable of the rich man and Lazarus, to the Pharisees; and the third, the parable of the unprofitable servant, to the apostles.

The lesson contained in the parable of the unjust steward (Luke 16:1-13) is frequently misunderstood, for it seems that Jesus commended the dishonesty of the steward. In this parable Jesus was teaching His followers that they were to have the responsibility of discharging a spiritual service to the people without His personal guidance. He was keenly aware that His disciples were still men of the world and not sufficiently acquainted with or trained in the principles of spiritual thinking and action. Jesus, therefore, depicted a trickster, a man well versed in methods used in the marts of trade where the dictum is that the end justifies the means. The unjust steward adhered faithfully to the only standard he knew. Jesus was not approving the dishonest act but was commending the consistency with which the steward operated. His god was mammon, whom he served devotedly and well. "The sons of this world are for their own generation wiser than the sons of the light" (Luke 16:8).

The persons who accept Jesus are called "sons of

light"; yet, are they as loyal to this higher standard as the "sons of this world" are to theirs? "If therefore ye have not been faithful in the unrighteous mammon, who will commit to your trust the true *riches?*" If the disciples had not complied with the best they understood before embarking on the spiritual way, how could they be trusted with a higher responsibility? They should not vacillate between the Christ idea and the world's ideal, for "no servant can serve two masters: for either he will hate the one, and love the other; or else he will hold to one, and despise the other. Ye cannot serve God and mammon."

And the Pharisees, who were lovers of money, heard all these things; and they scoffed at him. And he said unto them, Ye are they that justify yourselves in the sight of men; but God knoweth your hearts: for that which is exalted among men is an abomination in the sight of God (Luke 16:14, 15).

Then Jesus told the Pharisees the parable of the rich man and Lazarus (Luke 16:19-31). Charles Fillmore gives an interpretation of this parable as follows:

Jesus describes the states of consciousness of one who passes through the change called death. The rich man and Lazarus represent the outer and inner consciousness of the average worldly minded man and woman. The outer consciousness appropriates the attributes of soul and body and expresses them through sense avenues. "He was clothed in purple and fine linen, faring sumptuously every day." This condition typifies material riches.

Material selfishness starves the soul and devitalizes the psychical body. This body is described thus: "A certain beggar named Lazarus was laid at his gate, full of sores, and desiring to be fed with the *crumbs* that fell from the rich man's table." The soul life is put out of the consciousness and fed with the dogs.

When death overtakes such a one, the inner as well as the outer life changes environment. The material avenues are lost to the outer, and the soul finds self in a hell of desires without the flesh sensations through which to express itself. "And in Hades he lifted up his eyes, being in torments."

Lazarus, the beggar, was "carried away by the angels into Abraham's bosom." The inner spiritual ego, drawn by its innate spiritual ideas, finds a haven of rest in the bosom of the Father, represented by Abraham.

When man loses the material avenues of expression and has not developed the spiritual, he is in torment. Appetite longs for satisfaction, and in its anguish for a cooling draught, calls to its spiritual counterpart (Lazarus). But the body consciousness, the place of union for all the attributes of man, has been removed, producing in the life consciousness a great gulf or chasm that cannot be crossed, except by incarnation in another body.

Then the sense man is contrite, and would have his five brothers warned of the danger of sense life. These five brothers are the five senses. Abraham says, "They have Moses and the prophets; let them hear them"; that is, they understand the law (Moses) and they know what will follow its transgression (prophets). The rich man rejoins: "Nay, father Abraham: but if one go to them from the dead, they will repent." "And he said unto him, If they hear not Moses and the prophets, neither will they be persuaded, if one rise from the dead." The personal consciousness, which has been formed through material attachments, cannot be reached except through its own plane of consciousness. The phenomenal manifestations of spiritualism do not cause people to repent of their sins" (TT 155-157).

When the apostles were alone with Jesus they made a request of Him: "Increase our faith," they asked. To this He replied:

If ye had faith as a grain of mustard seed, ye would say unto this sycamine tree, Be thou rooted up, and be thou planted in the sea; and it would obey you (Luke 17:5, 6).

Jesus followed these words with the parable of the unprofitable servants (Luke 17:7-10). Its lesson is that no one is to be praised for doing what his work requires. "Even so ye also, when ye have done all the things that are commanded you, say, We are unprofitable servants; we have done that which it was our duty to do." Each of us has personal responsibilities to discharge, but if that is all we do, we are indeed "unprofitable servants." It is only when we go beyond the personal and fulfill our obligation to God in love, obedience, and service that we are rewarded with the faith that accomplishes mighty things.

While Jesus was still in Perea He received word from His beloved friends, Martha and Mary, that their brother Lazarus was sick. "When Jesus heard it, he said, This sickness is not unto death, but for the glory of God, that the Son of God may be glorified thereby" (John 11:4), and He remained in Perea two more days. Then, knowing that Lazarus had died, Jesus and His apostles went to Bethany (in Judea). The sorrowing sisters greeted Him. They believed that if Jesus had been with them Lazarus would not have died. Jesus said:

I am the resurrection, and the life: he that believeth on me, though he die, yet shall he live; and whosoever liveth and believeth on me shall never die (John 11:25, 26).

Then Jesus asked to be led to Lazarus' tomb, and He had the stone removed.

And Jesus lifted up his eyes, and said, Father, I thank thee that thou heardest me. And I knew that thou hearest me always: but because of the multitude that standeth around I said it, that they may believe that thou didst send me. And when he had thus spoken, he cried with a loud voice, Lazarus, come forth. He that was dead came forth, bound hand and foot with grave-clothes; and his face was bound about with a napkin. Jesus saith unto them, Loose him and let him go (John 11:41-44).

Of this outstanding miracle Charles Fillmore states:

Jesus represents man in the regeneration; that is, man in the process of restoring his body to its natural condition, where it will live perpetually without old age, disease, or death. A necessary step in this process of body restoration is the quickening of the sleeping Lazarus, who represents the vitalizing energies in the subconsciousness that feed the body and give it the life force that renews its youth. . . .

Bringing this sleeping life to outer consciousness is no easy task. Jesus groaned in spirit and was troubled at the prospect. The higher must enter into sympathy and love with the lower to bring about the awakening—"Jesus wept." But there must be more than sympathy and love —"Take ye away the stone." The "stone" that holds the sleeping life in the tomb of matter in subconsciousness is the belief in the permanency of present material laws. This "stone" must be rolled away through faith. The man who wants the inner life to spring forth must believe in the reality of omnipresent spiritual life and must exercise his faith in invoking in prayer the presence of the invisible but omnipresent God. . . .

In Spirit all things are fulfilled now. The moment a concept enters the mind, the thing conceived is consummated through the law that governs the action of ideas. . . . The spiritual-minded take advantage of this law and affirm the completeness of this ideal, regardless of outer appearances. This stimulates the energy in the thought process and gives it power beyond estimate. This is the step that Jesus took when He lifted up His eyes and said: "Father, I thank thee that thou heardest me. And I knew that thou hearest me always." The sleeping youth (Lazarus) does not at once respond, but the prayer of thanksgiving that is now in action gives the assurance that calls it at the next step to the surface—"Lazarus, come forth."

Jesus "cried with a loud voice." This emphasizes the necessity of working strenuously to project the inner life to the surface. . . .

Freedom from all trammels is necessary before the imprisoned life can find its natural channel in the constitution. "Loose him, and let him go" means unfettered life expressing itself in joyous freedom of Spirit (MJ 109-112).

Many Jews who were friends of the family had come to Bethany to be with Martha and Mary after Lazarus had died, and these witnessed his resurrection. Some of them believed that Jesus was indeed the Messiah, but others were antagonistic and reported the happenings to the Jewish leaders in Jerusalem. The Sanhedrin met promptly to consider how best to handle a situation that the members felt was rapidly getting out of hand. They could not deny the miracle but, on the other hand, they could not believe in the one who performed it. They dreaded Jesus' growing influence with the people, for they thought He would use His power to try to make Himself a king and thus cause a Roman army to be sent to Judea. Such action would, of course, endanger the Sadducees' political power. Finally Caiaphas, the high priest, said, "Ye know nothing at all, nor do ye take account that it is expedient for you that one man should die for the people, and that the whole nation perish not" (John 11:50). Definite plans to apprehend Jesus were set into operation, and from that time He lived with a price upon His head. He was not ignorant of what was going on, and withdrew to the village of Ephraim in the northern part of Judea. Here Jesus and His apostles remained until near the time for the Feast of the Passover, when He went through Samaria and into southern Galilee.

On the outskirts of one of the villages, Jesus and His apostles met a group of ten lepers. The Mosaic law required that lepers keep a certain distance from other persons and cry "unclean" when anyone approached them. When they saw Jesus the lepers pleaded, "Jesus, Master, have mercy on us" (Luke 17:13).

And when he saw them, he said unto them, Go and show yourselves unto the priests. And it came to pass, as they went, they were cleansed. And one of them, when he saw that he was healed, turned back, with a loud voice glorifying God; and he fell upon his face at his feet, giving him thanks: and he was a Samaritan. And Jesus answering said, Were not the ten cleansed? but where are the nine? Were there none found that returned to give glory to God, save this stranger? And he said unto him, Arise, and go thy way: thy faith hath made thee whole" (Luke 17:14-19).

In Jesus' time leprosy was a common disease, especially among the poorer classes. Since it was left to the priests to decide whether the victim was actually afflicted with leprosy or had some minor skin disease, only the priests could pronounce a leper clean and thus re-establish him in the community life. Jesus' command to the lepers that they show themselves to the priests was tantamount to saying that they were healed and would receive a clean bill of health from the proper authorities.

The spiritual significance of this miracle is that when we turn to the Christ Spirit within us and faithfully pray, we may be healed immediately. When we receive this blessing are we then so elated that we forget to thank God? If so, the healing is quite likely to be temporary, for we have failed to connect it with spiritual power. The leper who returned to glorify God was the only one whose permanent healing was certain. He knew the source from which it came and returned to express his gratitude.

Soon after His encounter with the ten lepers, Jesus gave two parables on prayer: the parable of the importunate widow (Luke 18:1-8) and the parable of the Pharisee and the publican (Luke 18: 9-14). The first stresses again the necessity of persistence in prayer. No analogy exists between the unjust judge and God, for God does not fail to answer prayer. He is never weary of our pleas. The lesson lies in the fact that we "ought always to pray, and not to faint," and in turning again and again to our Father we become responsive to the blessings He always has for us.

In the parable of the Pharisee and the publican Jesus draws a contrast between the prayer of the self-righteous individual and that of the humble penitent. The Pharisee was proud of his piety, which made him feel superior to other men. The publican offered his prayer in meekness of spirit. He was aware of his shortcomings and sought mercy. "I say unto you, This man went down to his house justified rather than the other: for every one that exalteth himself shall be humbled; but he that humbleth himself shall be exalted."

Jesus and His apostles soon left Galilee for the last time. Crossing the Jordan, they entered Perea, and it became known that Jesus was not to remain long. Many parents brought their children to Him "that he should lay his hands on them, and pray" (Matt. 19:13). When the apostles rebuked these parents for disturbing the Master, Jesus was indignant and said:

Suffer the little children to come unto me; forbid them not: for to such belongeth the kingdom of God. Verily I say unto you, Whosoever shall not receive the kingdom of God as a little child, he shall in no wise enter therein (Mark 10:14, 15).

After He had lovingly gathered the little children to Him, Jesus laid His hands on them and blessed them.

One day a young man of great wealth and high position came to Jesus. He was apparently convinced that Jesus could explain the meaning and mystery of life. He prostrated himself before the Master, crying, "Good Teacher, what shall I do that I may inherit eternal life?" (Mark 10:17). Jesus reminded him that only God is good, and asked if he were obeying the commandments. The young man assured Him that he was.

And Jesus looking upon him loved him, and said unto him, One thing thou lackest: go, sell whatsoever thou hast, and give to the poor, and thou shalt have treasure in heaven: and come, follow me (Mark 10:21).

With His marvelous power of discernment, Jesus saw that the young man's heart was attached to his riches, even though he had some desire for the things of Spirit. The prime requirement of spiritual living is to put God first, and that was the real meaning of Jesus' words to the young man. Jesus did not recommend poverty, but He always made it plain that spiritual attainment demands that love for God come first. When the young man "went away sorrowful: for he was one that had great possessions," Jesus said to His apostles:

Children, how hard is it for them that trust in riches to enter into the kingdom of God! It is easier for a camel to go through a needle's eye, than for a rich man to enter into the kingdom of God (Mark 10:24, 25).

Persons who have great wealth are apt to give more importance to it in their lives than they give to spiritual things. So long as they do they cannot attain godliness.

Peter reminded Jesus that the Twelve had "left all" and followed Him, and he questioned, "What then shall we have?" Jesus replied that those who had put personal interests aside "for my name's sake" shall "receive a hundredfold, and shall inherit eternal life. But many shall be last *that are* first; and first *that are* last" (Matt. 19:29, 30).

Since Jesus wanted to emphasize that God is no respecter of persons, and gives to all alike, He told the parable of the laborers in the vineyard (Matt. 20:1-16). Our heavenly Father is likened to the householder who is hiring laborers to work in His vineyard (God's workers in the world). To each of the persons who labored, even those who were hired the sixth, the ninth, and the eleventh hour, the householder gave the same pay—a shilling. The shilling represents all that man needs in the way of supply. It makes no difference when we accept Truth and begin to work with God. We may have known the joy of serving Him for many years, and yet the beginner in God's work may draw on the infinite resources of Spirit. People who have served God for a long time are sometimes apt to be envious of the good a beginner receives (the laborer who comes in at the eleventh hour), but the Lord says, "It is my will to give unto this last, even as unto thee." The true Christian will rejoice in this knowledge.

The time for the Feast of the Passover was approaching, and Jesus and His apostles joined a group of Galilean pilgrims who were on their way to Jerusalem. As they walked along the road, Jesus said to the Twelve:

> Behold, we go up to Jerusalem; and the Son of man shall be delivered unto the chief priests and scribes; and they shall condemn him to death, and shall deliver him unto the Gentiles to mock, and to scourge, and to crucify: and the third day he shall be raised up (Matt. 20:18, 19).

This was the most concise prophecy that Jesus had uttered, and the apostles still did not understand. Only a short time later, Salome, the mother of James and John, approached Him with the request that her sons sit "one on thy right hand, and one on thy left hand, in thy kingdom. But Jesus answered and said, Ye know not what ye ask. Are ye able to drink the cup that I am about to drink?" (Matt. 20:21, 22) meaning the trial He was to undergo. James and John answered that they were able, showing a complete lack of understanding of the events that were to come.

He saith unto them, My cup indeed ye shall drink: but to sit on my right hand, and on *my* left hand, is not mine to give; but *it is for them* for whom it hath been prepared of my Father (Matt. 20:23).

The Master knew that the apostles soon would suffer some of the things He had endured and was yet to endure. But neither He nor any other man could give them, nor can He give us today, the fruits of the kingdom. Glory and honor are for persons who attain the consciousness of oneness with God and receive from Him what He, in love, has prepared for them.

When the other apostles heard of the plea for special favors made on behalf of James and John, they were angry. Jesus, calling them to Him, gave the Twelve a lesson on spiritual greatness:

Ye know that the rulers of the Gentiles lord it over them, and their great ones exercise authority over them. Not so shall it be among you: but whosoever would become great among you shall be your minister; and whosoever would be first among you shall be your servant; even as the Son of man came not to be ministered unto, but to minister, and to give his life a ransom for many (Matt. 20:25-28).

In a spiritual sense a great person is one who is completely willing to serve, seeking not to be ministered unto but to minister to others. As he develops a consciousness of Spirit he takes on the qualities of Spirit, the chief of which is to pour itself out in service to mankind. "To give his life a ransom for many" does not refer to Jesus' crucifixion, but to the

great spiritual service He rendered during the years
of His ministry. He gave Himself unreservedly in
order that others could know the Truth that would
make them free.

As the pilgrims came near Jericho, Jesus was
accosted by a blind beggar whose name was Bartimæus. (Mark and Luke mention only one blind
man in their gospels, whereas Matthew's gospel men-
tions two. The miracles may be the same.) The
apostles tried to silence the beggar, but he continued
to cry out. Jesus then directed that Bartimæus be
brought to Him. When he was asked what he
wanted, the blind man replied, "That I may receive
my sight," and Jesus said, "Go thy way; thy faith
hath made thee whole" (Mark 10:52).

Metaphysically Bartimæus represents:

> A phase of the darkened mentality in man. This
> blinded, polluted, and poverty-stricken state of mind is
> the outcome of the race habit of attributing honor and
> precedence to old established beliefs and customs, to the
> exclusion of present spiritual inspiration. But this dark-
> ened, contaminated-with-error phase of the mentality is
> groping for light, which is realized through Jesus Christ,
> the Word of God expressed (MD 98).

It was necessary for travelers to rest at Jericho
before entering the dangerous, rocky, robber-haunted
gorge that led from it to Jerusalem. Jericho, near the
Dead Sea, is six hundred feet below the Mediterranean Sea level, and Jerusalem is nearly three thousand feet above it, necessitating an almost continuous
ascent for some six hours. A colony of publicans

was established in Jericho, and they collected revenues from persons who carried on a large traffic in buying and selling a kind of balsam that grew luxuriously in the hot, humid climate. The publicans also regulated the exports and imports between Judea, ruled by the Roman governor, and Perea, ruled by Herod Antipas. One of these chief publicans was the wealthy Zacchæus, a Jew, hated even by his own people for extorting exorbitant taxes from them. When Zacchæus heard that Jesus was passing through Jericho, he wanted to see Him. This presented a difficulty, however, for Zacchæus was short of stature and he could not see over the heads of the crowd that surrounded the Nazarene. Determined to see Jesus, Zacchæus climbed a sycamore tree, and as Jesus passed by He looked up and said to him, "Zacchæus, make haste, and come down; for to-day I must abide at thy house" (Luke 19:3). This Zacchæus did, and his contact with Jesus resulted in his complete reformation.

Behold, Lord, the half of my goods I give to the poor; and if I have wrongfully exacted aught of any man, I restore fourfold. And Jesus said unto him, To-day is salvation come to this house, forasmuch as he also is a son of Abraham. For the Son of man came to seek and to save that which was lost (Luke 19:8-10).

The name Zacchæus means "purified, just, righteous." These pertain to qualities that are the divine attributes of all men, but the character of a man may be perverted by an excessive love for material things.

Such a man becomes greedy and unjust. The mission
of the Christ is to save. When a person answers His
call, ("Zacchæus, make haste, and come down")
entertains Him, and listens to His word, a transformation takes place in his life ("the half of my goods
I give to the poor").

After they left Jericho, the apostles still thought
that Jesus was going to Jerusalem to set up the
kingdom of God on earth. It was at this time that
Jesus told them the parable of the pounds (Luke
19:12-27). Jesus represents the nobleman of the
parable, who is going away to receive a kingdom. He
will return; even though His countrymen hate Him
and oppose His rule. Nevertheless, He had given
each of His ten servants a gift (a spiritual quality
that is symbolized by a pound). Each servant was
to be rewarded in proportion to what use he made of
his gift. The servant who increased his gift was to
receive greater authority and also greater responsibility, while he who permitted his gift to lie dormant
was to be deprived of it.

This parable teaches that each one is given opportunity to take the gift of Truth that Christ gives.
The persons who accept Truth and abide by His
words (increase their gift) will develop their innate
spirituality, and their reward will be a greater understanding and spiritual power. Those who reject
Truth (refuse to use their gift) will lose their capacity for spiritual expression. "I say unto you, that
unto every one that hath shall be given; but from
him that hath not, even that which he hath shall be

taken from him" (Luke 19:26).

"And when he had thus spoken, he went on before, going up to Jerusalem" (Luke 19:28).

CHAPTER XI

Holy Week

THE GOSPELS VIVIDLY depict events that occurred in the last days of Jesus' earthly life. On Friday evening, six days before the Feast of the Passover, Jesus and the apostles arrived in Bethany and visited at the home of Lazarus, Martha, and Mary. Here many persons came, "not for Jesus' sake only, but that they might see Lazarus also, whom he had raised from the dead" (John 12:9).

On the following Sunday (which we now call Palm Sunday) Jesus and the Twelve left Bethany on foot to journey to Bethpage. As they neared the village Jesus sent two of the apostles on ahead, telling them to bring back a colt they would find there. The apostles did as they were instructed and, throwing their garments upon the colt, they put Jesus thereon. A multitude had now gathered, and the procession started for Jerusalem.

And the most part of the multitude spread their garments in the way; and others cut branches from the trees, and spread them in the way. And the multitudes that went before him, and that followed, cried, saying, Hosanna to the son of David: Blessed *is* he that cometh in the name of the Lord; Hosanna in the highest. And when he was come into Jerusalem, all the city was stirred, saying, Who is this? And the multitudes said, This is the prophet, Jesus, from Nazareth of Galilee (Matt. 21:8-11).

Jesus' ride into Jerusalem created quite a sensation, but it was a fulfillment of the prophecy of Zechariah: "Rejoice, greatly, O daughter of Zion; shout, O daughter of Jerusalem: behold, thy king cometh unto thee; he is just, and having salvation; lowly, and riding upon an ass, even upon a colt the foal of an ass" (Zech. 9:9). Jesus knew the prophecy, and this was His way of telling the people that He was their king and that He was just and lowly, even though He had brought salvation to the world through the word of God.

Metaphysically Jesus' action symbolizes the mastery of the I AM over the animal nature:

The characteristics of the ass are meekness, stubbornness, persistency, and endurance. To ride these is to make them obedient to one's will. The outer thoughts, or people, recognize that some unusual movement of mind is going on, and they fall into line. Their cry, "Hosanna," means *save now*. A change of base from personal willfulness to meekness and obedience stirs the whole consciousness, or city, and there is questioning about the cause. Simply saying in the silence, "Not my will, but thine, be done," often stirs up a commotion, and then there is questioning as to the cause. The answer is, "This is the prophet [one who states the spiritual law], Jesus [the I AM], from Nazareth [place of development] of Galilee" (life activity). Rendered in modern metaphysical terms this would read, "This is the supreme I AM stating the law of Spirit in development of life action (MD 348).

The Gospel of Luke gives additional information as regards the triumphal journey to Jerusalem. Some Pharisees were among the many persons who followed Jesus and, probably frightened by the enthusiastic shouts of the multitude, said to Him, "Master, rebuke thy disciples" (Luke 19:39). Jesus replied, "I tell you that, if these shall hold their peace, the stones will cry out" (Luke 19:40), meaning that it was indeed appropriate for the people to give honor to their Messiah and that even the inanimate stones would protest if the people were too blind to acclaim Him.

The procession could not proceed beyond the foot of Mount Moriah, upon which the Temple stood. Here the crowd dispersed, and Jesus and the apostles entered the Temple. "And the blind and the lame came to him in the temple; and he healed them" (Matt. 21:14). This, together with the people's cry, "Hosanna to the son of David," was the same as acknowledging Jesus as the Messiah.

The chief priests and scribes were so angry that they reprimanded Him. "Hearest thou what these are saying?" Jesus answered them adroitly, "Yea: did ye never read, Out of the mouth of babes and sucklings thou hast perfected praise"? (Matt. 21:16). Thus we find that spiritual Truth is often hid from the learned and revealed to the lowly who have more faith.

Sunday afternoon Jesus and the Twelve returned to Bethany. Here with their loved friends they spent the nights during Holy Week, walking to Jerusalem each day, a distance of about four miles.

On Monday morning, as Jesus and His companions set out for Jerusalem, He "hungered."

And seeing a fig tree by the way side, he came to it, and found nothing thereon, but leaves only; and he saith unto it, Let there be no fruit from thee henceforward for ever" (Matt. 21:19).

The barren fig tree symbolizes unfruitful conditions in our life. All of us need to bring forth the fruits of our spiritual nature, just as it is the function of the fig tree to produce figs. When we discover that a certain state of mind is not constructive and is the parent of unwholesome conditions, it is our right to "curse" or deny it. By the power of the word spoken in faith, we can "wither" these sterile states of mind and their attendant negative appearances and thus be free of them.

The apostles were surprised to see the fig tree dying immediately, and Jesus said to them:

Verily I say unto you, If ye have faith, and doubt not, ye shall not only do what is done to the fig tree, but even if ye shall say unto this mountain, Be thou taken up and cast into the sea, it shall be done. And all things, whatsoever ye shall ask in prayer, believing, ye shall receive (Matt. 21:21, 22).

Upon reaching the Temple, Jesus saw a scene He had witnessed three years before. There was great confusion. The outer court was crowded with merchants selling oxen, sheep, and doves. The money-changers were arguing with those who had foreign coins to exchange. Once again Jesus cleansed the Temple, saying, "Is it not written, My house shall be called a house of prayer for all the nations?

but ye have made it a den of robbers" (Mark 11:
17). The first cleansing of the Temple was at the
beginning of Jesus' ministry, the second cleansing
was just prior to His great test. This brings to mind
the thought that before we undertake any spiritual
project we should make certain that our consciousness is free of material beliefs and interests.

As Jesus was teaching in the Temple some
Greeks, probably Jewish proselytes attracted to Jerusalem by the Passover, asked Philip to arrange for
them to have a private interview with Jesus. Philip
was evidently puzzled at the request and told Andrew. Together the two apostles then informed Jesus
of the request. Historically, nothing is known of
these Greeks or why they wished to speak with
Jesus. Instead of granting their request, Jesus spoke
to the crowd at the Temple:

> The hour is come, that the Son of man should be glori-
> fied. Verily, verily I say unto you, Except a grain of wheat
> fall into the earth and die, it abideth by itself alone; but
> if it die, it beareth much fruit. He that loveth his life
> loseth it; and he that hateth his life in this world shall
> keep it unto life eternal. If any man serve me, let him
> follow me; and where I am, there shall also my servant
> be; if any man serve me, him will the Father honor (John
> 12:23-26).

Charles Fillmore states:

> Common sense often saves a man from the fanaticism
> of religious enthusiasm. The Greeks represent the practical
> side of man's nature. They ask Philip for an interview
> with Jesus, and Philip tells Andrew. All this means that

it is through the power (Philip) and strength (Andrew) in man that the sense reason acts, and when the I AM is called down from its lofty spiritual enthronement to the contemplation of practical life, there is a restoration of equilibrium. Then it recognizes the law of giving its exalted ideality to the earthly consciousness, that it may also be lifted up. To the higher consciousness this seems like the death of an ideal, but it is only a temporary submergence, which has its resurrection in a great increase of life and power. Thus we lose our life in the service of good, and count it of no value in order to find it again in Spirit (MJ 119).

In the higher consciousness we may realize that the surrender of the mortal way of thinking paves the way for the elevation of spiritual unfoldment, but such surrender is not easy for us. Even Jesus cried out, "Now is my soul troubled; and what shall I say? Father, save me from this hour" (John 12: 27). Yet even as the words left His lips there came the realization, "But for this cause came I unto this hour. Father, glorify thy name" (John 12:27, 28). When we have become established in spiritual consciousness, we understand that all we have striven for leads to the hour when only the Christ counts. Then our prayer is that the Father's name be glorified:

There came therefore a voice out of heaven, *saying,* I have both glorified it, and will glorify it again. The multitude therefore, that stood by, and heard it, said that it had thundered: others said, An angel hath spoken to him. Jesus answered and said, This voice hath not come for my sake, but for your sakes (John 12:28-30).

Thus a voice from heaven was heard the third time during Jesus' ministry. It had been heard at Jesus' baptism, and again on the mount of Transfiguration. It meant that "Jesus' heavenly credentials were sufficient and that there was nothing to fear. The demonstration must eventually be forthcoming" (MJ 120).

Now is the judgment of this world: now shall the prince of this world be cast out. And I, if I be lifted up from the earth, will draw all men unto myself (John 12:31, 32).

When we realize that Spirit is supreme, all the lingering falsity in our consciousness is dissolved (the prince of this world is cast out). As we lift up the Christ within, He draws to us all that is worthy of His presence.

The persons who heard these words did not understand, and Jesus, knowing the futility of attempting to explain further, only cautioned, "While ye have the light, believe on the light, that ye may become sons of light" (John 12:36). Yet many were not able to believe. A few who understood and would have accepted Him feared that the Pharisees would excommunicate them if their belief were known, and they still "loved the glory *that is* of men more than the glory *that is* of God" (John 12:43).

Again showing His divine authority, Jesus said:

He that believeth on me, believeth not on me, but on him that sent me. And he that beholdeth me beholdeth him that sent me. I am come a light into the world, that whosoever believeth on me may not abide in the darkness. And if any man hear my sayings, and keep them, I judge him not: for I came not to judge the world, but to save the world. He that rejecteth me, and receiveth not my sayings, hath one that judgeth him: the word that I spake, the same shall judge him in the last day" (John 12:44-48).

After speaking these words, Jesus and the Twelve left the Temple and returned to Bethany for the night.

When Jesus reached the Temple on Tuesday morning, He found a formidable deputation awaiting him. The chief priests, the learned scribes, and the leading rabbis were ready to challenge His authority as an accredited teacher. They bitterly resented Jesus' teachings, which were contrary to the established beliefs of Judaism as they interpreted them. They demanded to know by what authority He taught. Jesus knew they wanted to trap Him, so instead of answering their question, He asked one: "The baptism of John, whence was it? from heaven or from men?" (Matt. 21:25). This presented a problem to the Jews. If they admitted that John's baptism was "from heaven," that he was divinely inspired, they would be conceding that Jesus was the Messiah whom John had proclaimed. On the other hand, they dared not denounce John and say that his message was "of men," for the people reverenced the Baptist, and the rejection of John would stir up much antagonism. Thus the masters of Israel were reduced to the ignominious necessity of saying, "We know not" (Matt. 21:27). To this Jesus replied, "Neither tell I you by what authority I do these things" (Matt. 21:27). In this and in additional contests with His opponents, Jesus displayed a superhuman intelligence that enabled Him to perceive their machinations and to counteract them.

To drive home the lesson of their spiritual blindness, Jesus gave three parables: the parable of the two sons (Matt. 21:28-32), the parable of the wicked husbandmen (Matt. 21:33-43), and the parable of the wedding feast and wedding garment (Matt. 22:1-14). Each of these shows how the Jewish leaders had failed to discharge their spiritual obligations to God and man. They were indeed blind leaders of the blind. In their personal application these parables contain great lessons for us today.

The parable of the two sons is a reminder that it is what we do, not what we say, that is the measure of our worthiness. The first son represents persons who refuse to accept and live by a spiritual standard (decline to work in the Father's vineyard), but who later repent and obey Him. The second son typifies those persons who make a great boast of piety, yet do not honestly try to live righteously (they promise to work in the Father's vineyard but fail to do so). "Verily I say unto you, that the publicans and the harlots go into the kingdom of God before you" (Matt. 21:31).

The parable of the wicked husbandmen reveals that each of us is given charge of the divine resources of spirit, soul, and body. We must render an account of our stewardship to the Lord. If selfishness, greed, fear, and cruelty have been allowed to gain control over us, we try to retain our seeming good by repudiating the things of Spirit (slay the messengers of the Lord). However, the time comes when we are compelled to realize that the Christ is supreme (head of the corner) and that our rejection of Him leads to our utter defeat.

The parable of the wedding feast and the wedding garment relates that God has prepared a feast for all and invites us to it. Those in personal consciousness make light of His invitation, and they not only pursue their worldly interests but definitely reject His summons (kill the king's messengers). The price they pay is death to the good that God has for them. Those who accept His invitation must prepare themselves properly (wear a wedding garment). Our preparation for participation in God's good consists of spiritual thinking and living. The robe of righteousness is the only fit wedding garment. Without this, we shall not be permitted to eat at His table. "Bind him hand and foot, and cast him out into the outer darkness; there shall be the weeping and the gnashing of teeth. For many are called, but few chosen" (Matt. 22:14).

Though the Jewish authorities were enraged by Jesus' parables, the meaning of which was all too obvious to them, they had by no means exhausted their efforts to discredit Him. Certain Pharisees joined with a group of Herodians in questioning Him. The Herodians were a political party whose chief purpose was to uphold the reign of the Herods, whom the Pharisees despised. However, the Pharisees' hatred for Jesus was greater than their dislike for the Herodians and, in joining them, the Pharisees hoped that Jesus would be forced to make a statement that could be construed as disloyalty to Rome.

With words of flattery the Pharisees and Herodians approached Jesus:

> Teacher, we know that thou art true, and teachest the way of God in truth, and carest not for any one: for thou regardest not the person of men. Tell us therefore, What thinkest thou? Is it lawful to give tribute unto Cæsar, or not? But Jesus perceived their wickedness, and said, Why make ye trial of me, ye hypocrites? Show me the tribute money. And they brought unto him a denarius. And he saith unto them, Whose is this image and superscription? They say unto him, Cæsar's. Then saith he unto them, Render therefore unto Cæsar the things that are Cæsar's; and unto God the things that are God's (Matt. 22:16-21).

Again Jesus was more than a match for His enemies' attacks. His words are a guide for the perfect balance a person should have between worldly and spiritual things. We are to render unto each its rightful due. If we are faithful to God, we shall discharge our outer obligations rightly and without difficulty.

Completely routed, the Pharisees and Herodians retired. Then came a group of Sadducees with a query. Addressing Him with mock respect, they asked a trick question concerning the Resurrection, in which they themselves did not believe:

Teacher, Moses said, If a man die, having no children, his brother shall marry his wife, and raise up seed unto his brother. Now there were with us seven brethren: and the first married and deceased, and having no seed left his wife unto his brother; in like manner the second also, and the third, unto the seventh. And after them all the woman died. In the resurrection therefore whose wife shall she be of the seven? For they all had her. But Jesus answered and said unto them, Ye do err, not knowing the scriptures, nor the power of God. For in the resurrection they neither marry, nor are given in marriage, but are as angels in heaven. But as touching the resurrection of the dead, have ye not read that which was spoken unto you by God, saying, I am the God of Abraham, and the God of Isaac, and the God of Jacob? God is not *the God* of the dead, but of the living (Matt. 22:24-32).

Jesus' answer points out that the relationship of marriage as it is known on earth does not exist beyond the grave, "for in the resurrection they neither marry nor are given in marriage." Sex is of the flesh, and when the soul leaves the body, the latter disintegrates. God is not the God of the dead body, but of the living soul.

Yet, once more the insatiable spirit of dissension awoke, and this time a scribe, a student of the Torah, tried to fathom the extent of Jesus' wisdom:

Teacher, which is the great commandment in the law? And he said unto him, Thou shalt love the Lord thy God with all thy heart, and with all thy soul, and with all thy mind. This is the great and first commandment. And a second like *unto it* is this, Thou shalt love thy neighbor as thyself. On these two commandments the whole law hangeth, and the prophets (Matt. 22:36-40).

Jesus artfully combined the Ten Commandments into two. The Decalogue treats of man's right attitude toward God and his fellow man. The spiritual teaching of all the religious seers of the ages is summed up in these two commandments given by the Great Teacher. In the Sermon on the Mount Jesus had said, "Ye therefore shall be perfect, as your heavenly Father is perfect" (Matt. 5:48). We attain perfection by obedience to these two commandments.

Jesus now had the opportunity to question the Jewish leaders, and His query trapped them as they had hoped theirs would trap Him. He asked:

What think ye of the Christ? whose son is he? They say unto him, *The son* of David. He saith unto them, How then doth David in the Spirit call him Lord, saying,
The Lord said unto my Lord,
Sit thou on my right hand,
Till I put thine enemies under thy feet?

If David then calleth him Lord, how is he his son? (Matt. 22:42-45).

Jesus was quoting from the 110th Psalm, which the Pharisees regarded as distinctly Messianic; yet, they could think of no reply. There could be but one answer: the Son (Messiah) was divine, not human. Jesus was David's son by natural birth, since Mary was of the house of David. But as the Messiah, He was David's Lord. The Pharisees were embarrassed, since they could not explain a matter that concerned their own religion, and they withdrew.

Then spake Jesus to the multitudes and to his disciples, saying, The scribes and the Pharisees sit on Moses' seat: all things therefore whatsoever they bid you, *these* do and observe: but do not ye after their works; for they say, and do not (Matt. 23:1-3).

Jesus denounced formalism in religion in scathing words, and utterly repudiated the ambitious teachers, priests, and rabbis who care more for the praise of men than for obedience to God (Matt. 23:4-36). His was a call to recognize one God only. After He had enumerated the faults of a religion of the letter from which the Spirit had been banished, He termed it a mockery that was doomed to destruction. There was, however, more of grief than condemnation in His words, and He concluded with the heartfelt lament over the Holy City, whose sons had turned from the loving help that He would have given them so gladly and freely:

O Jerusalem, Jerusalem, that killeth the prophets, and stoneth them that are sent unto her! how often would I have gathered thy children together, even as a hen gathereth her chickens under her wings, and ye would not! Behold, your house is left unto you desolate. For I say unto you, Ye shall not see me henceforth, till ye shall say, Blessed *is* he that cometh in the name of the Lord (Matt. 23:37-39).

The day was now far advanced, and it was clear that any possibility of a reconciliation between Jesus and the Jewish leaders was gone. As He was leaving the Temple for the last time, He passed through the Court of the Women. In this court were thirteen chests, called "shoperoth," each shaped like a trumpet, into which the people were casting their contributions:

And he looked up, and saw the rich men that were casting their gifts into the treasury. And he saw a certain poor widow casting in thither two mites. And he said, Of a truth I say unto you, This poor widow cast in more than they all: for all these did of their superfluity cast in unto the gifts; but she of her want did cast in all the living that she had (Luke 21:1-4).

God does not require from us the sacrifice of material necessities, yet, when we love Him enough to deprive ourselves of some pleasure in order to support His ministry, our gift has much more worth than its monetary value. Likewise, it means more than the gifts of those who, from the abundance they have, share only a small portion. As we give freely in appreciation for the many blessings the Lord has bestowed on us, our consciousness expands and becomes a magnet for the attraction of additional good to ourselves. However, the expression "the widow's mite" has come to mean more than a contribution of money. It represents the giving of our all—love, obedience, service—in His name. This is what our Father asks of us. In return He gives unstintedly of Himself.

As Jesus and the apostles left the Temple, they turned and gazed once more at all its splendor. It was a magnificent structure, one of the wonders of the ancient world. The Temple had a number of beautiful gates. One was of solid Corinthian brass, and the others were overlaid with gold and silver. The building had graceful and towering porches, beveled blocks of marble, cloisters and stately pillars, with rising terraces of courts that led to the topmost court, the Holy of Holies. And as Jesus beheld this beauty, He was sad. He knew that little sincerity existed in the hearts of the majority of the worshipers, and without this the Temple could not be a house of prayer. It was already doomed, and He said to His companions, "See ye not all these things? verily I say unto you, There shall not be left here one stone upon another, that shall not be thrown down" (Matt. 24:2).

Forty years later this prophecy about the Temple was fulfilled literally, for in A.D. 70, the Roman general Titus had it completely destroyed. However, at the time that Jesus spoke, Judea was at peace with Rome. This prophecy apparently frightened the apostles, and they were silent as they left Jerusalem. After they had crossed the valley of Kidron, Jesus and the Twelve climbed the steep path that led to the Mount of Olives. When they had sat down to rest, the apostles asked, "Teacher, when therefore shall these things be? and what shall be the sign when these things are about to come to pass?" (Luke 21:7).

Jesus answered these questions in the Olivet Discourse, or the Great Eschatological Discourse, recorded in Matt. 24 and 25, Mark 13:1-37, and Luke 21:5-36. The language is metaphorical, and any attempt to interpret Jesus' words literally is vain. The phrase "end of the world" should be translated "consummation" (Emphatic Diaglott). Jesus was not predicting the destruction of this planet. He was referring to the dissolution of an age of mortal thought and the ushering in of a new era of spiritual understanding.

When we read this discourse we should keep in mind that Jesus was speaking to His apostles, the men who had been with Him as close companions during the three years of His ministry. They had at least some knowledge of the revolution in thought that results when a person applies Jesus' teaching. Those of us who are following Him in the regeneration know of the changes, often difficult, that take place with the passing of erroneous concepts and the coming of spiritual understanding. We should beware of false teachers who claim esoteric knowledge. We should wait in patience and faith for the Christ:

Then if any man shall say unto you, Lo, here is the Christ, or, Here! believe *it* not. For there shall arise false Christs, and false prophets, and shall show great signs and wonders; so as to lead astray, if possible, even the elect. Behold, I have told you beforehand. If therefore they shall say unto you, Behold, he is in the wilderness; go not forth: Behold, he is in the inner chambers; believe *it* not. For as the lightning cometh forth from the east, and is seen even unto the west; so shall be the coming of the Son of man (Matt. 24:23-27).

Jesus enumerated various tests that will be met

by spiritual aspirants. Even the "powers of the heavens shall be shaken," i.e., their faith and understanding shall waver. Let them stand firm, for such a shaking will precede spiritual realization and be "the sign of the Son of man in heaven" (Matt. 24: 29, 30).

And then shall all the tribes of the earth mourn, and they shall see the Son of man coming on the clouds of heaven with power and great glory. And he shall send forth his angels with a great sound of a trumpet, and they shall gather together his elect from the four winds, from one end of heaven to the other (Matt. 24:30, 31).

There has been much diversity of opinion on the second coming of Christ. Unity believes that Jesus' words should not be taken to mean that Jesus will again appear in the flesh. Had He not just said, "For as the lightning cometh forth from the east, and is seen even unto the west; so shall be the coming of the Son of man"? Surely the Christ, the Spirit of truth in man, shall make Himself known to those who are spiritually quickened. To them, Christ is indeed a living presence "with power and great glory." Charles Fillmore states:

The coming in the clouds of the heavens of the Son of man sitting on the right hand of Power . . . is the "second coming," and we should look nowhere else for the advent of the risen Christ. Christ is sitting today on the right hand of Power, which represents spiritual power expressed; the clouds of heaven being the obscurity in which sense consciousness holds the light of Truth.

Let us cease expecting Christ to come in bodily form;

let us turn our attention to His risen body already with us. In this way we shall co-operate with Him in setting up the kingdom of the heavens on the earth. . . .

The world needs the Christ consciousness now as never before. The need implies that the attainment is near at hand. There are men and women who gaze up into the heavens, looking for Christ, as did the early disciples, instead of looking within their own heart and mind. "Ye men of Galilee, why stand ye looking into heaven?" Only believe in the omnipresent Christ and you will behold Him sitting on the right hand of Power within your own being! (ASP 170, 171).

Jesus pointed out that numerous obstacles will be encountered in the process of spiritual unfoldment. Yet, He assures that these only indicate a greater degree of illumination in the future. When the branch of a fig tree becomes tender and puts forth leaves, then we know that summer is nigh (Matt. 24:32).

Verily I say unto you, This generation shall not pass away, till all these things be accomplished. Heaven and earth shall pass away, but my words shall not pass away. But of that day and hour knoweth no one, not even the angels of heaven, neither the Son, but the Father only. . . . Watch therefore: for ye know not on what day your Lord cometh (Matt. 24:34-42).

Jesus continued the discourse with four parables on preparedness: the parable of the master and the thief (Matt. 24:43, 44), the parable of the wise and evil servants (Matt. 24:45-51), the parable of the ten virgins (Matt. 25:1-13), and the parable of the talents (Matt. 25:14-30).

In the parable of the master and the thief, Jesus taught that we should always be on the alert to protect our spiritual consciousness (treasure). The mind of sense (thief) would steal or deprive us of faith, love, and wisdom. We should be in a spiritual consciousness at all times, "for in an hour that ye think not the Son of man cometh" (Matt. 24:44).

The parable of the wise and evil servants shows that our Lord has put us in charge of our being (His household) with instructions to tend and care for mind and body (our fellow servants). If enticements from the sense mind (evil servant) keep us from discharging our obligations, the law of God (Lord) will bring disaster to us, and "there shall be the weeping and the gnashing of teeth" (Matt. 24:51).

One of the most familiar parables is that of the ten virgins. They represent aspirants to spiritual wisdom and power (waited for the bridegroom). Five were wise. They had attained sufficient understanding to raise their senses to a spiritual level (had oil in their lamps) and were prepared for a greater illumination. The five foolish virgins had not gained the necessary knowledge or spiritualized their senses (had no oil in their lamps). When the time for illumination was at hand (the bridegroom arrived), the wise virgins received the joy and power that Christ gives (attended the wedding feast). The foolish virgins had to take time to procure the required understanding and to train their senses (go and buy oil) and were not on hand when the summons came to enter the new life. "Watch therefore, for ye know not the day nor the hour" (Matt. 25:13).

The parable of the talents is somewhat similar to the parable of the pounds, given earlier in Jesus' ministry. The Lord gives spiritual gifts (talents) to all of us. If these are used rightly they increase, and we receive additional blessings, "Well done, good and faithful servant: thou hast been faithful over a few things, I will set thee over many things; enter thou into the joy of thy Lord" (Matt. 25:21). When we fail to use our God-given abilities (hide our talents) through fear or neglect, the law (Lord) demands an accounting. The inevitable result is that we are deprived of what has been given to us. "Cast ye out the unprofitable servant into the outer darkness" (Matt. 25:30).

Jesus concluded the Olivet Discourse with the parable of the sheep and goats (Matt. 25:31-46). This parable portrays the action of man as he begins to realize his divine sonship ("when the Son of man shall come in his glory"). Our work now is to separate the true spiritual thoughts from the unredeemed vicious ones, even as a shepherd separates the sheep from the goats:

Then shall the king say to them on his right hand, Come, ye blessed of my Father, inherit the kingdom prepared for you from the foundation of the world: for I was hungry, and ye gave me to eat; I was thirsty, and ye gave me drink: I was a stranger, and ye took me in; naked, and ye clothed me; I was sick, and ye visited me; I was in prison, and ye came unto me. Then shall the righteous answer him, saying, Lord, when saw we thee hungry and fed thee? or athirst, and gave thee drink? And when saw we thee a stranger, and took thee in? or naked, and clothed thee? And when saw we thee sick, or in prison, and came unto thee? And the King shall answer and say unto them, Verily I say unto you, Inasmuch as ye did it unto one of these my brethren, *even* these least, ye did it unto me. Then shall he say also unto them on the left hand, Depart from me, ye cursed, into the eternal fire which is prepared for the devil and his angels: for I was hungry, and ye did not give me to eat; I was thirsty, and ye gave me no drink; I was a stranger, and ye took me not in; naked, and ye clothed me not; sick, and in prison, and ye visited me not. Then shall they also answer, saying, "Lord, when saw we thee hungry, or athirst, or a stranger, or naked, or sick, or in prison, and did not minister unto thee? Then shall he answer them, saying, Verily I say unto you, Inasmuch as ye did it not unto one of these least, ye did it not unto me. And these shall go away into eternal punishment: but the righteous into eternal life (Matt. 25:34-46).

The king may be likened to the Christ, the I AM which approves of our spiritual ideas and promises us all good, but condemns unworthy thoughts and warns us of trials ahead if we indulge in negative thinking. There is nothing to fear in this judgment if we preserve our divine ideas and deny error thoughts:

We are carried along by these thoughts [all types of thoughts] until we reach the consciousness of our I AM power. We do not know we are building ourselves, our environment, our world, until we reach this consciousness. Then judgment of our world begins and is passed on our thought creations. Suppose we have tried to cast the beam out of our eye so that we might help our brother. This act will answer in our judgment day. "I was that 'least' one." . . .

All things are in the consciousness, and you have to learn to separate the erroneous from the true, darkness from light. The I AM must separate the sheep from the goats. This sifting begins right now and goes on until the perfect child of God is manifest and you are fully rounded out in all your Godlike attributes (ASP 48, 49).

On Tuesday evening, as Jesus and the apostles walked toward Bethany in the twilight, He again reminded them of His coming trial: "Ye know that after two days the passover cometh, and the Son of man is delivered up to be crucified" (Matt. 26:2).

The events of this day, when Jesus had so completely baffled His opponents, led to a meeting of the Sanhedrin that night. The consensus of this meeting was that Jesus must be taken in secret, but that His capture should wait until after the Passover to prevent an uprising among the people in His behalf.

While the meeting in Jerusalem was going on, Jesus reached Bethany:

So they made him a supper there: and Martha served; but Lazarus was one of them that sat at meat with him. Mary therefore took a pound of ointment of pure nard, very precious, and anointed the feet of Jesus, and wiped his feet with her hair: and the house was filled with the odor of the ointment (John 12:2, 3).

Judas objected to this, for he considered it a waste, and said, "Why was not this ointment sold for three hundred shillings, and given to the poor?" (John 12:5). Jesus replied, "Suffer her to keep it against the day of my burying. For the poor ye have always with you; but me ye have not always" (John 12:7, 8).

Mary represents the devotional aspect of man, which is filled with love for the Christ. The anointing of Jesus' feet symbolizes the willingness of love to serve. Judas typifies the sense thought, which is filled with selfishness. "The Judas consciousness believes in poverty and has no understanding of the true law of supply. All that comes into consciousness is selfishly appropriated and dissipated by this thief, yet he produces nothing" (MJ 116). Jesus' words, "The poor ye have always with you; but me ye have not always," mean that our service to the downtrodden is laudable, but there are likewise times when an expression of love should be given to our Lord. We are not always aware of Him ("me ye have not always") but when we are aware of Him, the precious ointment of our devotion should be freely spent on Him. If we have a true prosperity consciousness, we know that one type of giving need not curtail us in any other form of helpfulness.

What motive prompted Judas to bargain with the Jews to betray Jesus? Perhaps he was stung by the Master's rebuke. Perhaps Judas felt that Jesus' cause was now lost and that he should salvage what he could from three years of following the Galilean. Or perhaps Judas thought that the betrayal would bring matters to a climax and force Jesus to declare

Himself to be the Messiah. Whatever the motive, Judas went to Jerusalem that very night, sought out the Jewish authorities, and asked what they would pay him to deliver Jesus to them. They offered him thirty pieces of silver, the price of the meanest slave, and Judas agreed. Metaphysically,

Judas represents the unredeemed life forces. He also typifies that in humanity which, though it has caught the higher vision of life, still resorts to underhanded methods in order to meet its obligations. . . .

Judas also symbolizes desire, appropriation, acquisitiveness. Acquisitiveness is a legitimate faculty of the mind, but covetousness is its Judas. When acquisitiveness acts within the law it builds up the consciousness. Exercised in its native realm, the free essences of Being, it draws to us the supplies of the universe and through it we enter into permanent possessions. But when it oversteps the law it is a destroyer. . . .

And so we find among our disciples, or faculties, this one whose tendency is such that through it we are brought into condemnation and suffering. It is known from the first; it is Judas, self-appropriation. . . . It is through the exercising of this faculty that suffering and crucifixion are brought about. It is the faculty that draws to us the substance of things. While in its essence it is good, yet if one appropriates it in its personal sense, "good were it for that man if he had not been born." . . .

Judas is transformed and redeemed when all pertaining to personality is surrendered and the substance of divine love is poured into consciousness. Man is continually enriched as he gives up the things of sense and consecrates himself to purity of purpose (MD 375, 376).

After the intense activity of Sunday, Monday, and Tuesday, Jesus apparently remained in Bethany on Wednesday. Nothing is known of His activity on this day. Undoubtedly He spent it in prayer, preparing for the crucial test that He knew He was soon to meet.

CHAPTER XII

The Last Supper and Gethsemane

O N THURSDAY, the day before the beginning of the Feast of the Passover, Jesus ate the paschal meal with His apostles. To partake of this meal had long been the custom of the Jews.

The word *paschal* means "pertaining to the Passover," and refers especially to the paschal lamb that was slain by the priests and brought from the Temple to be roasted. The lamb was the main dish of the meal. The other food requirements were unleavened bread, wine, water, bitter herbs, and a sauce called *charosheth.* This meal, preceeding the Feast of the Passover, carried out the ideas of sacrifice and redemption, and was eaten in remembrance of the lamb that was slain to protect the Israelites from the scourge of death at the time of their liberation from Egyptian bondage (see *Exod. 12*). Jesus is frequently referred to as the Paschal Lamb. This is because He gave His life for the redemption of mankind.

On the day of the paschal meal the apostles asked Jesus where the preparations were to be made for this meal. Selecting Peter and John, Jesus asked them to go to Jerusalem.

Behold, when ye are entered into the city, there shall meet you a man bearing a pitcher of water; follow him into the house whereinto he goeth. And ye shall say unto the master of the house, The Teacher saith unto thee, Where is the guest-chamber, where I shall eat the passover with my disciples? And he will show you a large upper room furnished: there make ready (Luke 22:10-12).

This was the last meal that Jesus ate with the Twelve before the Crucifixion, and it has come to be known as the Last Supper. In all probability it took place in the home of the parents of John Mark. This home served as a rendezvous for the disciples after the Crucifixion, and it was here that the Holy Spirit came to them on the day of Pentecost. Spiritually, the upper room signifies "the high state of mind that we assume in thinking about spiritual things. It may be attained through prayer, or by going into the silence with true words, or in spiritual meditation" (MD 668).

After Peter and John had made the proper preparations for the supper they returned to Bethany. In the evening Jesus and the Twelve arrived at the house in Jerusalem and retired to the upper room. In his book, "The Life of Christ," Frederick W. Farrar presents an interesting view of the scene:

When they arrived the meal was ready, the table spread, the triclinia [mats] laid with cushions for the guests. Imagination loves to reproduce all the probable details of that deeply moving and eternally sacred scene, and if we compare the notices of ancient Jewish custom, with the immemorial fashions still existing in the changeless East, we can feel but little doubt as to the general nature of the arrangements. They were totally unlike those with which the genius of Leonardo da Vinci and other great painters has made us so familiar. The room probably had white walls, and was bare of all except the most necessary furniture and adornment. The couches or cushions, each large enough to hold three persons, were placed around three sides of one or more low tables of gaily painted wood, each scarcely higher than stools. The seat of honor was the central one of the central triclinium or mat. This was, of course, occupied by the Lord. . . . At the right hand of Jesus reclined the beloved disciple [John], whose head therefore could, at any moment, be placed upon the breast of his friend and Lord.

As Jesus and the apostles took their places, there arose contention among the Twelve, probably as regards the seating arrangements. Jesus reminded them of their true position, saying:

> The kings of the Gentiles have lordship over them; and they that have authority over them are called Benefactors. But ye *shall* not *be* so: but he that is the greatest among you, let him become as the younger; and he that is chief, as he that doth serve. . . . I am in the midst of you as he that serveth (Luke 22:25-28).
>
> And during supper . . . *Jesus,* knowing that the Father had given all things into his hands, and that he came forth from God, and goeth unto God, riseth from supper, and layeth aside his garments; and he took a towel, and girded himself (John 13:2-4).

Then He washed the feet of the apostles. It was the custom in those days for a person entering a house to take off his sandals so as not to bring in dust or dirt from the road. The apostles had done this, but they had neglected to wash their feet. Generally the host had a servant perform this service for guests. As Jesus continued this menial task, awe and shame silenced the apostles, until Jesus came to Peter, who protested:

> Thou shalt never wash my feet. Jesus answered him, If I wash thee not, thou hast no part with me. Simon Peter saith unto him, Lord, not my feet only, but also my hands and my head. Jesus saith to him, He that is bathed needeth not save to wash his feet, but is clean every whit: and ye are clean, but not all. For he knew him that should betray him; therefore said he, Ye are not all clean. . . . Know ye what I have done to you? Ye call me, Teacher, and, Lord: and ye say well; for so I am. If I then, the Lord and the Teacher, have washed your feet, ye also ought to wash one another's feet. . . . Verily, verily, I say unto you, A servant is not greater than his lord; neither one that is sent greater than he that sent him. If ye know these things, blessed are ye if ye do them (John 13:8-17).

Peter's attitude of self-abnegation would serve to keep him from union with Spirit. The Christ always serves, and we cannot be too proud in the personal consciousness to refuse to accept His service. Jesus said, "If I wash thee not, thou hast no part with me." Peter comprehended something of the depth of Jesus' meaning when he made his plea, "Lord, not my feet only, but also my hands and my head." This was not necessary, for Jesus knew that Peter had begun the regeneration, and his understanding (represented by the feet) needed additional cleansing. The symbolic meaning of washing another's feet is that, as Jesus' followers, it is our duty to serve men by helping them to cleanse their consciousness of false beliefs and thus bring to them the light of true understanding.

As Jesus resumed the meal He was "troubled in the spirit" and said, "One of you shall betray me" (John 13:21). The apostles did not know of whom He spoke, and Peter leaned over and asked John to find out. John was reclining on the couch next to Jesus with his head on Jesus' breast. "Lord, who is it?" he inquired. Jesus answered:

He it is, for whom I shall dip the sop, and give it him. So when he had dipped the sop, he taketh and giveth it to Judas, *the son* of Simon Iscariot (John 13:26).

Handing a sop to someone was not unusual, for at Eastern meals the guests ate out of a common bowl. A guest would dip a piece of bread into the bowl, take up a portion of meat, and then pass it to another guest. Judas, however, understood Jesus' action, and "then entered Satan into him." Jesus said to Judas, "That thou doest, do quickly" (John 13:27), and Judas, in haste, left the room. The other apostles did not understand what Jesus said to John, and they thought that the Master had sent Judas on an errand.

Then Jesus said:

Now is the Son of man glorified, and God is glorified in him . . . Little children, yet a little while I am with you. Ye shall seek me, and as I said unto the Jews, Whither I go, ye cannot come; so now I say unto you, A new commandment I give unto you, that ye love one another . . . By this shall all men know that ye are my disciples, if ye have love one to another (John 13:31-35).

Peter insisted on knowing where Jesus would go.

When Jesus replied that Peter could not accompany Him now but would follow Him later, Peter asked, "Lord, why cannot I follow thee even now? I will lay down my life for thee" (John 13:37). Peter represents faith, and faith is very sure of itself at times. But Jesus knew that faith, until it is made completely steadfast by spiritual realization, is changeable. He warned His loving yet fickle follower: "The cock shall not crow, till thou hast denied me thrice" (John 13:38).

And as they were eating, Jesus took bread, and blessed, and brake it; and he gave to the disciples, and said, Take, eat; this is my body. And he took a cup, and gave thanks, and gave to them, saying, Drink ye all of it; for this is my blood of the covenant, which is poured out for many unto remission of sins (Matt. 26:26-28).

In the Gospel of Luke these words are added: "This do in remembrance of me" (Luke 22:19). The Holy Communion has become a sacrament of the Christian church. Unity teaches that the bread represents divine substance and that the wine represents divine life. We are to eat and drink these; that is, we are to appropriate the substance and life of Christ through affirmative prayer. *"Through Christ I now partake of divine substance. Through Christ I now partake of divine life."* When we contemplate the divine ideas of substance and life our consciousness is charged with them and we assimilate them. The result is the lifting of the soul to a spiritual level. Unity does not believe that communion is an

act performed only in church on Sunday, and it does
not use the symbols of bread and wine. Unity holds
that true communion may be entered into when we
turn our attention to Christ and declare His substance and life active in us now. Communion is the
form of prayer in which we seek at-one-ment with
Christ. Charles Fillmore states:

The Christ substance (body) and the Christ life
(blood) are accessible at all times and in all places to the
one who awakens his I AM to spiritual omnipresence. The
table of the Lord is spread everywhere for those who believe on Him as Spirit and in their Spirit affirmation eat of
His body and blood. The appropriation by His followers
of His life and substance is the very foundation of salvation through Jesus Christ. The mere acceptance intellectual-
ly of the teaching that we are saved by the blood of the
Lord Jesus and the partaking of the bread and wine in a
perfunctory manner will save neither soul nor body. The
only thing that will do it is the understanding that Jesus
raised His body life and substance out of the race consciousness into Spirit consciousness and that with our mind
poised in that consciousness we can lay hold of the Spirit
elements that will save us to the uttermost (JC 158, 159).

While He was still in the upper room Jesus spoke
the comforting words recorded in the 14th chapter
of John. He knew the apostles would have trials to
meet after He had left them and He said:

Let not your heart be troubled: believe in God, believe
also in me. In my Father's house are many mansions; if it
were not so, I would have told you; for I go to prepare a
place for you. And if I go and prepare a place for you, I

come again, and will receive you unto myself; that where I am, *there* ye may be also (John 14:1-3).

Even as we believe in God, we should also believe in the Christ, God's manifestation in us. When we do, human anxiety passes. "Many mansions" means many abiding places. "The meaning of Jesus was that He was making a permanent abiding place for those who believed in His teaching and accepted Him for what He really was—God manifest. . . . The permanent abiding place to which Jesus invites His friends is 'prepared' by Him: He makes the place Himself; in fact, He is the place" (MJ 130). We may always abide where He is by acknowledging His presence.

"And whither I go ye know, and the way ye know." Thomas protested that the apostles knew neither where Jesus was going nor the way. "I am the way, and the truth, and the life: no one cometh unto the Father, but by me," said Jesus (John 14:6). There is only one way to spiritual realization (the Father) and that way is through obedience to the Jesus Christ teaching. Then Philip asked that the apostles be shown the Father, and Jesus answered:

Have I been so long time with you, and dost thou not know me, Philip? he that hath seen me hath seen the Father . . . Believest thou not that I am in the Father, and the Father in me? the words that I say unto you I speak not from myself: but the Father abiding in me doeth his works (John 14:9, 10).

When we come into an understanding of our

spiritual nature, our oneness with the omnipresent
principle of life, the Father is revealed. "The Father
principle may be so developed in man that it will
move him unerringly in all his ways, and the Father
may even speak words through his mouth. When this
point is reached, the question of man's unity with
the Father principle is wholly removed, the manifestation of wisdom and power in him proving that a
higher principle is at work through him" (MJ 131).

Verily, verily, I say unto you, He that believeth on me,
the works that I do shall he do also; and greater *works*
than these shall he do; because I go unto the Father. And
whatsoever ye shall ask in my name, that will I do, that
the Father may be glorified in the Son. If ye shall ask anything in my name, that will I do (John 14:12-14).

When, through faith, we have made union
with the Christ Mind, we shall be able to do the
works that Jesus performed, and even "greater
works." We shall be granted "whatsoever ye shall
ask in my name." His name stands for spiritual man
(Christ), and to ask in the realization of the indwelling Christ is to open our consciousness to the infinite good that is resident in Spirit. Persons have
asked in His name in a literal sense and have not
received. Prayer must be substantiated by spiritual
realization if we are to have the fulfillment of the
promise.

If ye love me, ye will keep my commandments. And I
will pray the Father, and he shall give you another Comforter, that he may be with you for ever, *even* the Spirit of

truth: whom the world cannot receive; for it beholdeth him not, neither knoweth him: ye know him; for he abideth with you, and shall be in you. I will not leave you desolate: I come unto you. Yet a little while, and the world beholdeth me no more; but ye behold me: because I live, ye shall live also. In that day ye shall know that I am in my Father, and ye in me, and I in you. He that hath my commandments, and keepeth them, he it is that loveth me; and he that loveth me shall be loved of my Father, and I will love him, and will manifest myself unto him (John 14:15-21).

Charles Fillmore's interpretation of these verses is:

In this Scripture Jesus, representing the I AM, gives assurance of divine co-operation to those who are loyal in thought and word to the Truth. You now know the relation in which you stand to the Father. Spiritually you are one, but to sustain this spiritual relation until it is fully manifested in your body and environment requires attention. The concrete aspect of Truth, represented by the personality of Jesus, must be taken away before you can understand Truth in its abstract or universal sense. Then withdrawing your attention from the letter or personality and centering it upon Truth in its spiritual essence, you will find that there is an intelligible side to that which seemed vague and indefinite. The Comforter, the Advocate, the Spirit of truth is omnipresent as divine wisdom and power, which are brought into active touch with our consciousness through our believing in Him. In "the world"—on the phenomenal side—we cannot know this guide and helper, but having learned the truth about the omnipresence of Spirit, with all the abundance of life, love, Truth, and intelligence through which it is made manifest, we at once begin to realize that the Mighty One dwells with us, and "shall be in you" (MJ 133, 134).

Continuing His discourse Jesus said:

These things have I spoken unto you, while *yet* abiding with you. But the Comforter, *even* the Holy Spirit, whom the Father will send in my name, he shall teach you all things, and bring to your remembrance all that I said unto you (John 14:25, 26).

Unity believes in the trinity of Father, Son, and Holy Spirit, and interprets the Father as Principle, or God. The Son is the expression of God in the individual, namely, the Christ, or I AM. The Holy Spirit is called the Comforter or the Spirit of truth. Charles Fillmore says: "The Holy Spirit is neither the all of Being nor the fullness of Christ, but is an emanation, or breath, sent forth to do a definite work." The Holy Spirit is perhaps best understood as the "executive power of both Father and Son, carrying out the creative plan" (TT 134).

"Peace I leave with you; my peace I give unto you: not as the world giveth, give I unto you. Let not your heart be troubled, neither let it be fearful. . . . Arise, let us go hence" (John 14:27, 31).

With this beautiful benediction ringing in their ears the apostles silently followed Jesus from the room. While they walked along the road toward the garden of Gethsemane, Jesus told them of the need for a closer union with Him if they were to bring forth spiritual fruits. He clothed His lesson in the allegory of the vine and the branches:

I am the true vine, and my Father is the husbandman. Every branch in me that beareth not fruit, he taketh it away: and every *branch* that beareth fruit, he cleanseth it, that it may bear more fruit. Already ye are clean because of the word which I have spoken unto you. Abide in me, and I in you. As the branch cannot bear fruit of itself, except it abide in the vine; so neither can ye, except ye abide in me. . . . He that abideth in me, and I in him, the same beareth much fruit: for apart from me ye can do nothing (John 15:1-5).

When we attempt to live without recognizing our dependence on the indwelling Christ, we are like a branch severed from the vine and receiving no nourishment. Charles Fillmore says:

When our faith attaches itself to outer things, instead of the spiritual I AM, it ceases to draw vitality from the one and only source of life, Divine Principle. The only door to this life is the I AM. This abiding is a conscious centering of the mind in the depths within us by means of repeated affirmations of our faith and trust in it. This day-by-day repeating of affirmations finally opens a channel of intelligent communication with the silent forces at the depths of Being, thoughts and words flow forth from there, and an entirely new source of power is developed in the man (MJ 138).

In concluding this particular teaching Jesus reminded the apostles that even as the Father loved Him, so He in turn loved them: "Abide ye in my love. . . . These things have I spoken unto you, that my joy may be in you, and *that* your joy may be made full. This is my commandment, that ye love one another, even as I have loved you" (John 15:9-12).

It is not difficult for us to "abide" in Jesus when we love Him and know that He loves us. As we abide in Him, we may feel His joy and appropriate it for ourselves. Then we can obey what is sometimes referred to as the eleventh commandment, namely, that we love one another "even as I have loved you."

Jesus warned the apostles of persecutions that would come. "If they persecuted me, they will also persecute you" (John 15:20). He urged them to remember what He had said. It was expedient for Him to leave them, "for if I go not away, the Comforter will not come unto you; but if I go, I will send him unto you" (John 16:7). So long as we depend on a person, no matter how spiritual he may be, we do not find the Spirit of truth (Comforter) within ourselves. Each of us must make his own spiritual demonstration and should not lean on anyone, even on Jesus as a man. We find our own Christ self by adhering to Jesus' teaching and it is then we realize that the spiritual presence of Jesus has been with us all the time, and that without Him our search would have been fruitless.

The apostles did not understand Jesus' prediction: "A little while, and ye behold me no more; and again a little while, and ye shall see me" (John 16:16). He was referring to the Crucifixion and the Resurrection. The first would separate Him from them, and the second would bring Him back to them. However, they did realize that some great change was about to take place when He said, "I came out from the Father, and am come into the world: again, I leave the world, and go unto the Father" (John 16:28). Jesus had no fear of coming events, for He knew that it was in His power to overcome anything the world could inflict on Him.

As Jesus and the apostles drew near Gethsemane, Jesus lifted up His eyes and prayed what is known as the Prayer of Intercession. There are three distinct parts to the prayer: the first part for Himself, the second for the apostles, and third for future believers:

Father, the hour is come; glorify thy Son, that the Son may glorify thee: even as thou gavest him authority over all flesh, that to all whom thou hast given him, he should give eternal life. And this is life eternal, that they should know thee the only true God, and him whom thou didst send, *even* Jesus Christ. I glorified thee on the earth, having accomplished the work which thou hast given me to do. And now, Father, glorify thou me with thine own self with the glory which I had with thee before the world was (John 17:1-6).

Charles Fillmore states:

In this Scripture Jesus was asking of the Father as never before. To glorify means to magnify with praise, to enhance with spiritual splendor, to adorn. Jesus was asking for a full and complete unification of His consciousness with that of the Father. Jesus realized that He had been given all authority over the flesh. He was holding the realization not only for His own glorification but also for that of His disciples. Jesus realized that in this union a full understanding of God and His laws would be revealed, which would naturally make clear to Him the way of eternal life (MJ 147).

In praying that He would be glorified with the

glory that He had had with the Father "before the world was," Jesus was recognizing the Christ as eternal and existing in full consciousness of wholeness before there had been a manifest world.

His prayer for the apostles was made in the realization that the Father had given them to Him to instruct in His word, and "they have kept thy word" (John 17:6). "Holy Father, keep them in thy name which thou hast given me, that they may be one even as we are" (John 17:11). While with them He had instructed the apostles in spiritual things, and they were lifted above worldly thoughts. Now He prayed not that they be taken from the world, but that they be preserved from the "evil *one*" (worldly consciousness). "Sanctify them in the truth: thy word is truth. As thou didst send me into the world, even so sent I them into the world" (John 17:17, 18).

The third and last portion of the Prayer of Intercession was for those who "believe on me through their word" (John 17:20). He asked that they too be able to recognize their oneness with the Father and with Him, "even as thou, Father, *art* in me, and I in thee, that they also may be in us: that the world may believe that thou didst send me" (John 17:21). Through them God's word was to be given to many, and Jesus prayed "that the love wherewith thou lovedst me may be in them, and I in them" (John 17:26).

In proportion as people understand and have faith in Jesus Christ as their actual Saviour from sin, and in proportion as they are set free from appetite, passion, jealousy, prejudice, and all selfishness, they experience wholeness of mind and body as the result. The ultimate result of this knowledge and of daily practice in overcoming (even as Jesus Himself overcame) will be a new race that will demonstrate eternal life—the lifting up of the whole man —spirit, soul, and body—into the Christ consciousness of oneness with the Father. This is indeed true glorification. By means of the reconciliation, glorification, and at-onement that Jesus Christ re-established between God and man, we can regain our original estate as sons of God here upon earth (MJ 149).

The tones of this intercessory prayer faded away, and Jesus and the Eleven arrived at the garden of Gethsemane. At the gate He stopped and motioned to Peter, James, and John to accompany Him. He bid the others, "Sit ye here, while I go yonder and pray" (Matt. 26:36). As He and the three moved away He said to them, "My soul is exceeding sorrowful, even unto death: abide ye here, and watch with me" (Matt. 26:38). Alone, He went farther into the garden and there He fell on the ground, praying, "My Father, if it be possible, let this cup pass away from me: nevertheless, not as I will, but as thou wilt" (Matt. 26:39).

Many persons believe that the will of God for each man is health, abundance, peace, and joy. When these things are not in evidence, it is right to pray for them. However, the greatest prayer that any man can utter is "not as I will, but as thou wilt." There comes a time to each of us in our spiritual ongoing when the lesser good should be overshadowed by the greater. Our goal is nothing less than the realization of complete oneness with God. This is Christ mastery. We may shrink from what appears to be a difficult test, and we may cry, "Let this cup pass away from me," but our surrender to God's will is all that is necessary to insure the outworking of His good.

After His prayer Jesus returned to the three apostles and found them sleeping: "What, could ye not watch with me one hour? Watch and pray, that ye enter not into temptation: the spirit indeed is willing, but the flesh is weak" (Matt. 26:40, 41). Twice more Jesus prayed the same prayer. Twice more He returned to find the apostles sleeping. After the third time He was completely at peace. Looking again on the slumbering men, He said:

> Sleep on now, and take your rest: behold, the hour is at hand, and the Son of man is betrayed into the hands of sinners. Arise, let us be going: behold, he is at hand that betrayeth me (Matt. 26:45, 46).

Jesus' praying in the garden represents:

The struggle that takes place within the consciousness when Truth is realized as the one reality. All the good is pressed out and saved and the error is denied away. This is often agony—the suffering that the soul undergoes in giving up its cherished idols or in letting go of human consciousness.

The great work of everyone is to incorporate the Christ Mind in soul and body. The process of eliminating the old consciousness and entering into the new may be compared to Gethsemane, whose meaning is *oil press* . . . a press is an emblem of trial, distress, agony, while oil points to Spirit and illumination (MD 231).

Several hours had passed since Judas left the upper room where the Last Supper was held. He had gone to the high priest and had indicated that this was the time to turn Jesus over to the Jews. The high priest gave Judas an escort of armed men, and Judas, knowing where Jesus was likely to be, led them to the garden of Gethsemane. He gave his companions a sign, saying, "Whomsoever I shall kiss, that is he; take him, and lead him away safely" (Mark 14:44). On approaching Jesus, Judas greeted Him and kissed Him.

Jesus knew that He would be betrayed, but He made no effort to defeat the act of Judas. Sense consciousness betrays man every day, yet it would be unwise to destroy it before its time, because at its foundation it is good. Man is continually enriched as he gives up the things of sense and consecrates himself to purity of purpose.

Defense seemed useless, especially as Jesus made no effort to save Himself, and the apostles stood helplessly by; that is, all but Peter. Peter, the impulsive, drew a sword and severed the ear of Malchus, a servant of the high priest. Instantly Jesus rebuked Peter:

Put up again thy sword into its place: for all they that take the sword shall perish with the sword. Or thinkest that I cannot beseech my Father, and he shall even now send me more than twelve legions of angels? (Matt. 26:52, 53).

Jesus then touched the ear of Malchus and it

was healed. Malchus, the high priest's servant, symbolizes the limited understanding and judgment of the ruling power that the high priest represents. Peter's cutting off Malchus' right ear may be interpreted as meaning that we should not use our faith destructively. Such a proceeding would only serve to further limit the possibilities of a person's perceiving and laying hold of Truth. Jesus' healing the ear shows that limited understanding and judgment should be healed, illumined, and lifted up instead of being pushed still farther into unreceptivity and darkness.

The men who had come with Judas to take Jesus had not known what to expect. When they saw that Jesus had no intention of resisting arrest, they seized and bound Him. No doubt the apostles were overcome with surprise and distress upon being confronted by a multitude armed with "swords and staves." "Then all the disciples left him, and fled" (Matt. 26:56). Thus alone, Jesus was led a captive to the palace of the high priest, Caiaphas.

CHAPTER XIII

Trials and Crucifixion

AFTER JESUS had been seized, bound, and placed in the custody of Jewish officials He was given two trials—one religious and the other civil. In each there were three stages. The religious trial consisted of His appearance before Annas; then before Caiaphas and an informal committee made up of members of the Sanhedrin; and last, an appearance before a regular meeting of this court. The civil trial took place first before Pontius Pilate; then before Herod Antipas, tetrarch of Galilee and Perea; and then again before Pilate. No one Gospel contains the full information about these trials, but by putting the various events in the four accounts together, the whole story is related.

The reason for this double legal procedure was that, although the Sanhedrin could try both civil and religious cases affecting the Jews, it could not give an order for the execution of a prisoner on whom it had passed the death sentence. Only the Roman procurator, Pontius Pilate, had this power. Therefore, when the Sanhedrin condemned Jesus to death, it had to ask Pilate to issue the order for crucifixion. Crucifixion was a Roman form of execution. If the Sanhedrin had been able to inflict the death penalty, Jesus would have been stoned.

Jesus was taken first to Annas. Annas had been the high priest before Caiaphas, his son-in-law, was appointed, and he still was the real power in the

Sanhedrin. John 18:19-24 records the proceedings of
the first stage of Jesus' trial, which began before
dawn on Friday morning.

When Annas questioned Jesus about His teachings, Jesus said that He had preached openly in the
synagogues and the Temple where the Jews came
together, and that He never had taught in secret. He
suggested that Annas question those who had heard
Him preach as regards His teachings. Annas felt that
this answer was disrespectful, and he sent Jesus to
Caiaphas, who had hurriedly called together some
of the members of the Sanhedrin. The account is reported in Matthew 26:59-68 and Mark 14:55-65.
Two witnesses testified falsely against Jesus, saying
that He had claimed superhuman power. Jesus did
not answer the charges, and Caiaphas demanded:

> I adjure thee by the living God, that thou tell us
> whether thou art the Christ, the Son of God. Jesus saith
> unto him, Thou hast said: nevertheless I say unto you,
> Henceforth ye shall see the Son of man sitting at the right
> hand of Power, and coming on the clouds of heaven (Matt.
> 26:52, 53).

Cries of "blasphemy" rang through the room,
and the assembled Jews declared that He deserved
to die.

While Jesus was appearing before Annas and
Caiaphas, Peter and John came to the high priest's
residence. John knew the high priest and gained ad-
mittance, but Peter was stopped at the door. In the
court outside the residence, a group of servants were

warming themselves by a fire of coals. Peter joined them, and at different times three persons asked if he were not the friend of the Galilean prisoner. Each time Peter denied that he knew Jesus. Just as the third denial left Peter's lips, Jesus was led across the court to the guardhouse to await the formal meeting of the Sanhedrin. Thus, Jesus heard His boldest apostle's repudiation of Him, and He looked straight at Peter. Immediately a cock crowed, and "Peter remembered the word which Jesus had said, Before the cock crow, thou shalt deny me thrice. And he went out, and wept bitterly" (Matt. 26:75).

Peter's denial of Jesus shows us that while spiritual faith is being developed in consciousness it is often changeable and wavering:

Until faith is thoroughly identified with the Christ, you will find that the Peter faculty in you is a regular weathercock. It will in all sincerity affirm its allegiance to Spirit, and then in the hour of adversity will deny that it even knew Spirit. This, however, is in its probationary period. When you have trained it to look to Christ for all things, under all circumstances, it becomes the stanchest defender of the faith (MD 517).

According to Jewish law, a legal meeting of the Sanhedrin could not be held before sunrise, which would be about six o'clock. At that time, Jesus was led before the Sanhedrin, the supreme court of the Jews, the majority of whose members were determined that He should die. The account is recorded in Luke 22:66-71.

As in the informal trial before Caiaphas, only

one charge was brought against Jesus—blasphemy. When asked if He were the Son of God, Jesus replied, "Ye say that I am. And they said, What further need have we of witness? for we ourselves have heard from his own mouth" (Luke 22:70, 71). Their next action was to take Jesus to Pilate with the request that He be executed.

The religious trial of Jesus "shows how a merely formal religion will persecute and attempt to kill the inner Christ Spirit and all that pertains to it" (MJ 154).

Doubtless Judas had kept himself posted on all that occurred. When he heard the decision of the Sanhedrin and knew that Pilate would be asked to pronounce the death sentence, Judas realized fully what he had done. Hastening to the chief priests, he attempted to return the thirty pieces of silver he had received for betraying Jesus, saying, "I have sinned in that I betrayed innocent blood" (Matt. 27:4). The priests would not take the money, and Judas, in an agony of remorse, threw down the silver in the sanctuary and "went away and hanged himself" (Matt. 27:6).

The death of Judas signifies the dissolution of the unredeemed life forces that betray us, and makes way for the lifting up of the forces that will aid us in laying hold of spiritual life. Matthias, whose name means "given wholly unto Jehovah," was later selected to replace Judas as an apostle.

The Jewish leaders took Jesus to Pilate. The fullest account of the first appearance of these leaders and Jesus before the Roman procurator is given in John 18:28-38. When Pilate asked the Jews what charge they preferred against the prisoner, they poured forth a volley of accusations. The chief one was that Jesus set Himself up as a king. The Sanhedrin had condemned Him for blasphemy, but such a charge would have been ignored by Pilate, who cared nothing for the religion of the Jews. Therefore, a charge that would represent Jesus as a threat to the Roman government had to be invented.

Instead of condemning Jesus unheard, Pilate questioned Him privately: "Art thou the King of the Jews?" he asked. Jesus replied:

My kingdom is not of this world . . . Thou sayest that I am a king. To this end have I been born, and to this end am I come into the world, that I should bear witness unto the truth. Everyone that is of the truth heareth my voice. Pilate saith unto him, What is truth? And when he had said this, he went out again unto the Jews, and saith unto them, I find no crime in him (John 18:36-38).

Pilate represents:

The ruling principle of the sense plane, the carnal will. Pilate questioned the I AM, Jesus, "Art thou the King of the Jews?" Applying this to the individual man, one would say to oneself, "Is there a ruling will over my religious nature?" The personal will has no concept of the factors of that inner higher realm, and believes that it is the ruler of the whole man. It is jealous of any attempt to usurp its power, but when it is assured that the kingdom that the higher self would rule is "not of this world," it finds in that self "no fault" (MD 530).

The Jews greeted Pilate's verdict with anger and
insisted that Jesus was a disturber of the peace.
When he learned that Jesus was a Galilean, Pilate
thought to rid himself of a troublesome case by
sending Him to Herod Antipas, tetrarch of Galilee,
who was then in Jerusalem to attend the Passover.

The account of Jesus' appearance before Herod
is given in Luke 23:6-12. Herod was pleased to see
Jesus, as he had heard many reports of His miracles
and wanted to witness one. "And he [Herod] questioned him [Jesus] in many words; but he answered
him nothing" (Luke 23:9). The Jews standing by
continued to accuse Jesus. Herod, evidently angered
by Jesus' silence, allowed the soldiers to mock Him
and, in derision of His supposed kingly role, they
arrayed Him in a gorgeous robe and sent Him back
to Pilate. Herod passed no sentence on Jesus.

The third stage of the civil trial is recorded in
each Gospel. The most detailed account is given in
John 18:39, 40 and 19:1-16. Pilate's duty was to
acquit Jesus, since he had turned the case over to
Herod, tetrarch of the territory in which Jesus lived,
and Herod had dismissed Him. Pilate tried to acquit
Him by telling the Jews that neither he nor Herod
had found Jesus guilty of any crime that was worthy
of death. It was the custom for Rome to release
a Jewish prisoner during the Passover, and Pilate
suggested that Jesus be released. Pilate wanted to
save an innocent man and at the same time appease
the Jews, but they would not hear of it. "Not this
man, but Barabbas," (John 18:40) they shouted.

Barabbas was a robber and the leader of a recent revolt against Rome, yet the people chose to release him instead of Jesus. As a last resort, and hoping that the Jews' wrath might be satisfied by scourging Jesus, Pilate gave Him over to the Roman soldiers for scourging. After the soldiers had done this, in derision they placed a crown of thorns on His head, "and arrayed him in a purple garment" (John 19:2), calling Him "King of the Jews!"

And Pilate went out again, and saith unto them, Behold, I bring him out to you, that ye may know that I find no crime in him. Jesus therefore came out, wearing the crown of thorns and the purple garment. And *Pilate* saith unto them, Behold, the man! (John 19:4, 5).

Perhaps Pilate's words, "Behold the man," implied that he thought Jesus' punishment had been sufficient and that he was returning the man they had brought to him. Or perhaps Pilate's words meant that he recognized the greatness of Jesus and in admiration acknowledged the Man among men.

However, the Jewish leaders, together with the rabble they had incited, cried, "Crucify *him*." When Pilate still demurred, the Jews brought up their real charge against Jesus—that He called Himself the Son of God. Again Pilate questioned Jesus, and again he wished to free Him. But the Jews, in desperation, said: "If thou release this man, thou art not Cæsar's friend; every one that maketh himself a king speaketh against Cæsar" (John 19:12). This was the subtle insinuation to Pilate that by protecting Jesus he was harboring a traitor to the Roman government. If such a report were relayed to Rome, it would undoubtedly cause serious trouble for Pilate and could even mean his death. He therefore gave the order for the crucifixion of Jesus, making it clear to the Jews that he considered himself "innocent of the blood of this righteous man" (Matt. 27:24).

The trial of Jesus, resulting in the Crucifixion, symbolizes a man who is controlled by human consciousness. Pilate gave the order under duress. The innate sense of justice that is present in all men was in the case of Pilate violated by the Jewish leaders' insistence that Jesus be executed. Pilate himself was not emotionally involved in the situation and, therefore, his finer instincts and his understanding had opportunity to assert themselves. The Jews, on the other hand, had what they considered a just case. The Pharisees hated Jesus because they considered Him a menace to their religion; the Sadducees wanted Him out of the way because they considered Him an agitator who threatened their political and economic security. Thus, both Jewish parties were emotionally involved, and their sense of justice was obscured. Their fault was spiritual blindness. Our attitude toward those who caused the crucifixion of Jesus should be one of compassion rather than condemnation. The main points of Jesus' teaching are that we love God and our fellow man, but in order to do this a certain degree of spiritual understanding and development is necessary. As Christians we are endeavoring to attain this spiritual level now by releasing all criticism and prejudice and by striving to manifest the Christ virtues of forgiveness, tolerance, and love.

After the Roman soldiers had again mocked Jesus they stripped Him of the purple robe, put on Him His own garments, and a cross was laid on His shoulders. According to the historian Plutarch, it was customary for a criminal to carry his cross to the place of execution. "And there were also two others, malefactors, led with him to be put to death" (Luke 23:32).

Golgotha (Calvary in its Latin form), a well-known site just outside the gates of Jerusalem, was selected as the place for the Crucifixion. The word *Golgotha* means "a place of the skull," and Charles Fillmore states:

The seat of the conscious mind is the front brain, and there the will has established its dominion. There all things affecting the body are either admitted or rejected. Even spiritual Truth has to be admitted through this door before it can become part of the consciousness. It is there that the human will must be crossed out, to give the divine will free expression (MD 240).

Jesus had come through a terrific ordeal, having been scourged, mocked, and buffeted by His accusers, and as the procession made its way toward Golgotha, He tottered under the weight of the Cross. Simon, a man of Cyrene who was bound for Jerusalem, was compelled by the soldiers to bear the Cross for Jesus.

Among the crowd that followed Jesus were many

women who lamented His plight. Jesus admonished
them not to weep for Him. No matter how severe
the suffering is that comes to us, we should remember that we shall pass through the valley of the shadow in safety if we remain steadfast in faith. But
Jesus made a stern prediction of impending disaster
for the Jews. In days of distress they shall long for
death and "then shall they begin to say to the mountains, Fall on us; and to the hills, Cover us" (Luke
23:30).

When the procession reached Golgotha, and before Jesus was put on the Cross, the Roman soldiers
offered Him "wine mingled with myrrh" (Mark
15:33). Crucifixion was the cruelest form of execution, and it was an evidence of compassion on the
part of the executioners that they customarily gave
those who were to be crucified a draught of wine
medicated with a powerful narcotic to dull the ex-
cruciating pain. "But he [Jesus] received it not"
(Mark 15:23). He chose to be in full control of all
His faculties. The Crucifixion was to be the crucial
moment of His life. He would meet it with the Father, of whose love and mercy He was confident.

On Friday morning at the "third hour" (nine
o'clock) the crosses were raised. Jesus was in the
middle, with a thief on each side. On a white wooden
tablet above His head the words, "JESUS OF NAZ-
ARETH, THE KING OF THE JEWS," were written in Latin, Greek, and Hebrew. This was Pilate's
way of inflicting public scorn on the Jews. Immediately a committee called on Pilate with the request

that the inscription be removed, but Pilate was adamant and said, "What I have written I have written" (John 19:22).

The Roman soldiers stripped Jesus of His garments and divided them. However, when they saw His coat they agreed not to tear it but to cast lots for its possession. The coat, or seamless robe as it is generally called, was a beautiful and valuable garment "without seam, woven from the top throughout" (John 19:23). It represents:

The truth in its harmonious expression and unchangeable perfection.

Regeneration forms a new mind and a new body consciousness. . . . The seamless coat of Jesus symbolizes a consciousness of the indestructible unity of life and substance in the body consciousness. This consciousness inheres in the executive department of mind (soldiers), and can be exercised by Spirit in body projection when so desired (MD 153).

The scene was one of tumult. Many of the watchers stood by silently. Some mocked Jesus, bidding Him come down from the Cross and save Himself. Likewise, the chief priests and scribes taunted, "He saved others; himself he cannot save" (Mark 15:31).

The Crucifixion symbolizes the crossing out of all that belongs to the mortal consciousness in order that the way may be made for the coming forth of the Christ self. Jesus' seven last words (or sayings) on the Cross symbolize steps that should be taken in the final overcoming of the mortal mind.

No one Gospel records all of Jesus' seven last words. Each gives either one or three of them, and Bible scholars have arranged them in sequential order.

During the first three hours after Jesus was placed on the Cross He spoke three times. In these words He fulfilled His entire obligation to man: first, by forgiving His enemies; second, by promising mercy to the repentant sinner; and third, by discharging His responsibility to His mother.

"Father, forgive them; for they know not what they do" (Luke 23:34).

This saying was addressed to His persecutors and reveals His forgiving love. Unforgiveness is a most destructive emotion, and it is based on a lack of understanding. Persons who are unjust to us "know not what they do," for injustice breeds injustice for those who perpetrate it. We should pray for these persons. By doing this we enter into the Christ forgiveness that cleanses us of the injustices we have committed unconsciously or deliberately.

"To-day thou shalt be with me in Paradise" (Luke 23:43).

Jesus' cross was between those of the two malefactors. One of these taunted Him, "Art not thou the Christ? save thyself and us" (Luke 23:39). The other reprimanded him, saying that they indeed were receiving their just desert but that Jesus was an innocent man. Turning to Jesus, the repentant man said, "Remember me when thou comest in thy kingdom" (Luke 23:42), and Jesus made him the great promise, "To-day shalt thou be with me in Paradise." Whenever we turn to Christ, confess our sins, and ask His help, it is always freely given. Through His grace, we shall enter into paradise (consciousness of peace and wholeness).

"Woman, behold thy son! . . . Behold, thy mother!" (John 19:26, 27).

Jesus addressed these words to Mary and the apostle John, who were standing near the cross. Thus He fulfilled His responsibility to His mother, and tradition states that Mary lived with John for the remainder of her life. Jesus' action reminds us that it is our duty to provide for those who have a right to expect provision from us. To discharge our human responsibilities willingly and lovingly is a definite part of spiritual unfoldment.

Jesus was to be on the Cross for three more hours, from noon until shortly after three in the afternoon. During these hours there was "darkness over the whole land," and Jesus was silent until just before three o'clock. At that time He uttered a cry of desolation and physical anguish.

"My God, my God, why hast thou forsaken me?" (Mark 15:34).

By giving expression to this universal sense of aloneness in trial Jesus released it for Himself and for us. Experiencing crucifixion spiritually, an erasing of all sense thought and feeling, is difficult when we face it. During this trying time we may feel that even God has forsaken us. When these periods of darkness and doubt come, we should remember that

Jesus passed through a similar period. We should remember also that it was comparatively momentary for Him and will be for us. The challenge is to persevere until the demonstration is completed.

"I thirst" (John 19:28).

This is the cry of the body and symbolizes physical distress of every kind. There comes a time in spiritual unfoldment when we must know that the body is not limited to the physical. It is composed of divine substance and activated by divine intelligence. It is the temple of the Lord, and its full needs can be met only by drinking of the living water (the word of Christ). Jesus voiced the demand of the body for Himself and us, and we should remember that if we remain stanch in faith our body shall be lifted to spiritual perfection.

Near the Cross stood a jar that contained a sour wine (vinegar) from which the Roman soldiers had drunk. When Jesus said, "I thirst" one of them took a sponge and filling it with the liquid, raised it to Jesus' lips. Jesus accepted this simple act of mercy. Almost immediately He spoke the words that revealed the heights to which His consciousness had risen.

"It is finished" (John 19:30).

Jesus' suffering was now almost over. His work was finished. His mission was to show man "the way, and the truth, and the life," and this had now been accomplished. Henceforth for Him the limited kingdom of earth would be supplanted by the finished kingdom of God. When we undergo a severe trial and keep the faith, we finally come to the place of knowing that every vestige of human effort is exhausted. God is in control. Our release is very near. This release came to Jesus, and it will come to us when the seventh or last word is spoken:

"Father, into thy hands I commend my spirit" (Luke 23:46).

In complete surrender to the Father, Jesus' prayer "not my will, but thine, be done," was answered. The life of Spirit was on the march, and victory was its only outcome. When we give ourselves fully to Him, the last barrier between the personal and the spiritual is dissolved. The way is open then for His action to take place in us, and He cannot fail.

When Jesus spoke this last word, He "gave up his spirit" (John 19:30). At that moment the veil of the Temple was rent in two from the top to the bottom:

The last step in regeneration is the giving up of the thought of the corporeal existence of the body temple. Then the veil of sense thought that conceals the spiritual body is rent, and man comes into consciousness of the body imperishable and eternal (MD 673).

An earthquake shook the earth and split the rocks, and even the Roman soldiers were no longer indifferent. In awe they exclaimed, "Truly this was the Son of God" (Matt. 27:54).

At the crucifixion of Jesus it was the human consciousness of a perishable body that died. "Our old man was crucified with *him,* that the body of sin might be done away, that so we should no longer be in bondage to sin." When the thoughts of sin and death are crossed out, the spiritual truth about life and its manifestation in the body takes form in consciousness (MD 348).

The Sabbath began at sunset on Friday, and the Jews wanted the bodies of the three men taken down from the crosses before that time. They went to Pilate with the request that the legs of the men be broken to hasten their deaths. The Roman soldiers did this to the two thieves, but when they came to Jesus they discovered that He was dead. To make absolutely sure, one of them drove a spear into His side.

Joseph of Arimathaea, a prominent Jew and a member of the Sanhedrin, and secretly a follower of Jesus, asked Pilate for Jesus' body for burial. The request was granted, and with the help of Nicodemus, Joseph wrapped the body in linen and laid it in a new tomb in his garden. A huge stone was then rolled to the entrance of the tomb. By the time the men had completed their ministrations it was sunset, and the Sabbath had begun.

The crucifixion of Jesus became the foundation of the Christian doctrine of salvation by the blood of Jesus. Christians generally believe that Jesus gave His blood on the Cross as a sacrifice for the sins of every person, and that when one accepts Him as Saviour one is saved by His blood. The Jews have always believed that sin was expiated through sacrifice and that the blood of the slain animal on the altar cleansed man of sin. Jesus has been considered the "sacrificial lamb" who was killed to bring about a reconciliation of sinful man to God.

Unity accepts this doctrine, but gives it a different interpretation. Unity believes that we are saved by appropriating His blood, which represents spiritual life. Charles Fillmore says:

Jesus raised the blood of His body to spiritual potency. This purified blood was sown as seed in our race thought and can be appropriated by anyone who raises his thoughts to those of Jesus. This is accomplished through faith in Jesus to save from sin, to inspire one with His Spirit, or through asking Jesus to come to the aid of the sin-sick mind or suffering body. A single atom of the purified blood of Jesus can begin a vitalizing and purifying work in mind and body that will continue until the Christ man appears (KL 28).

The doctrine of the vicarious atonement is also associated with Jesus' crucifixion. Unity teaches that Jesus did indeed make an atonement for man, not by His death but by His life, His teaching, and His final overcoming of death. Prior to the ministry of Jesus mankind had been held in the bondage of limitation by erroneous beliefs and consequent sins:

We can readily see how a whole race might be caught in the meshes of its own thought emanations and, through this drowsy ignorance of the man ego, remain there throughout eternity, unless a break were made in the structure and the light of a higher way let in. This is exactly what has happened to our race. In our journey back to the Father's house we became lost in our own thought emanations, and Jesus Christ broke through the crystallized thought strata and opened the way for all those who will follow Him.

By so doing He made a connection between our state of consciousness and the more interior one of the Father —He united them—made them a unit—one, hence the at-one-ment or atonement through Him. He became the way by which all who accept Him may "pass over" to the new consciousness of all mortal beliefs that hold us in bondage—such as sin, evil, sickness, fleshly lusts, and death —which He overcame. "I have overcome the world." Jesus' "overcoming" made a great rent in the sense consciousness, and opened a way by which all who desire may demonstrate easily and quickly (TT 165, 166).

In order for us to take advantage of the atonement Jesus made for us, it is imperative that we follow Him. "Keep my word," He said. This means that we are to take on His ideas, speak His word, and do the things that He did. He set an example and He showed that whatever He urged others to do He could do. He taught love by showing love. He taught forgiveness by forgiving those who despitefully used Him. He admonished, "Seek ye first his kingdom and his righteousness" and made that search the first consideration of His life. His is the greatest service ever rendered to humanity, for He released the Christ consciousness to the world. The only way we can unify ourselves with the Christ is:

By centering our mind upon Jesus and silently asking His help in our demonstrations. It is not the prayer of a "worm of the dust" to a god, but of one who is on the way of asking guidance of one who has passed over the same road, and who knows all the hard places and how to get through them.

This in one sense is the relation of Jesus Christ to each of us, and so far as our present demonstration is concerned, it is the most important relation. The road that we are traveling from the mortal plane of consciousness to the spiritual plane is beset with many obstructions, and we need the assistance of one stronger than any of those who now dwell in flesh bodies. He who is still in the perception of the earthly is not always a safe guide, because he sees in a limited way. We want one who sees wholly in Spirit, and such a one we find in Jesus Christ (TT 168, 169).

CHAPTER XIV

Resurrection, Appearances, and Ascension

THE JEWISH SABBATH that immediately preceded the Resurrection in A.D. 30 must have been a time of stress and strain for the followers of Jesus. No record can be found of the whereabouts of the apostles during this time, but several of the women who had stood at the Cross saw where Jesus had been laid. They watched at the tomb until the Sabbath began. Then they retired to their homes for rest, in accordance with the Jewish custom.

Shortly after the Crucifixion the chief priests went to Pilate and insisted that Jesus' tomb be guarded for three days. They recalled the rumored prophecies of His resurrection and were afraid that His disciples would steal the body and spread abroad the report that Jesus had risen from the dead. Pilate granted their request. The tomb was sealed, and a Roman guard was left to watch it.

Within the tomb man's greatest overcoming was taking place.

The three days that Jesus was in the tomb represent the three movements of mind that are involved in overcoming error. First, nonresistance and humility; second, the taking on of the divine activity, or receiving the will of God; third, the assimilation and fulfillment of the divine will (MD 349).

Jesus had already accomplished the demonstration over the last enemy, death, when, at dawn on the first day of the week, Mary Magdalene, Mary the mother of James, and Salome hastened toward the sepulchre. They had prepared spices and ointments to anoint Jesus' body, and as they approached the garden where Jesus was buried, they wondered, "Who shall roll us away the stone from the door of the tomb?" (Mark 16:3). The women did not know that the tomb had been sealed and guarded. They did not know that there had been an earthquake and that the stone no longer barred the entrance to the tomb.

For an angel of the Lord descended from heaven, and came and rolled away the stone, and sat upon it. His appearance was as lightning, and his raiment white as snow: and for fear of him the watchers did quake, and became as dead men (Matt. 28:2-4).

As they reached the tomb the women were amazed to see that the stone had been rolled away and that an angel sat there. The angel said:

Fear not ye; for I know that ye seek Jesus, who hath been crucified. He is not here; for he is risen, even as he said. Come, see the place where the Lord lay. And go quickly, and tell his disciples, He is risen from the dead (Matt. 28:5, 6).

The angel represents the spiritual I AM.

The first affirmation of the I AM for its body is that it is not under any limitation of material thought; that it is free with the freedom of Spirit. "He is not here; for he is risen." The second affirmation of the I AM for its body is a swift and universal proclamation of omnipresence and activity in all realms of consciousness. "Go quickly, and tell his disciples, He is risen" (MD 349).

In a tumult of rapture and excitement the women hurried back to Jerusalem and told the apostles what they had seen and heard. The men were incredulous, but when Mary Magdalene went to Peter and John privately with her news, they ran to the burying place. John outran Peter, but the former did not enter the tomb first. When Peter arrived, he went into the tomb and found the linen cloths and the napkin that had covered the body of Jesus. Then John entered and saw that the tomb was empty. Faith (Peter) is often more courageous than love (John), but both see and believe.

The apostles and the women seemed to have forgotten Jesus' promise that He would rise from the dead.

It is not at all surprising that the very near friends of Jesus were filled with astonishment and fear when they found that He was not in the tomb where He had been laid. They could not understand that for years He had been training His soul to accomplish this very thing. But He had spent whole nights in prayer, and through the intensity of His devotions had made union with Divine Mind. This union was so full and so complete that His whole being was flooded with spiritual life, power, and substance, and the wisdom to use them in divine order. In this manner He had projected the divine-body idea, and through it His mortal body was transformed into an immortal body.

This was accomplished before the Crucifixion, and Jesus knew that He had so strengthened His soul that it would restore His body, no matter how harshly the body might be used by destructive man (MJ 172, 173).

Jesus had declared, "I am the resurrection, and the life" (John 11:25), and He substantiated this declaration by raising His body. As the Way-Shower, it was necessary for Him to prove that the body can be so transformed that it triumphs over death.

The resurrection is the lifting up of the whole man into the Christ consciousness. The whole man is spirit, soul, and body. The resurrection lifts up all the faculties of mind until they conform to the absolute ideas of Divine Mind, and this renewal of the mind makes a complete transformation of the body so that every function works in divine order and every cell becomes incorruptible and immortal (MD 554).

Jesus' promise to each of us is, "He that believeth on me, though he die, yet shall he live" (John 11:25). This means that although man, through ignorance, has developed destructive states of mind that are expressed as restricting conditions, he may, through faith in Christ, overcome them and live a new and better life. "And whosoever liveth and believeth on me shall never die" (John 11:26) is the remainder of this promise. This means that those who live in harmony with spiritual laws shall, through continued faith, be able to attain eternal life. The cardinal point of Charles Fillmore's teaching is that each person should bend every effort toward this goal, and he says, "eternal life means con-

tinuous conscious existence in the body" (TT 151).
It is inevitable that as the consciousness of man is
spiritualized so is his body. We have before us constantly the example of Jesus who, by complete
obedience to God, used His body for the right purpose—a temple of the living God. Mr. Fillmore further states:

Having a body of spiritually electrified atoms, Jesus is
able to quicken the bodies of people who attract His presence by believing in Him; He radiates a glorious life that
energizes those who believe in His power.

By positive affirmations we must all appropriate this
same Christ life, substance, and Truth as ours individually
and as the very foundation and substance of our body.

Thousands in this day have found the law that Jesus
demonstrated and the inner meaning of the Truth that He
taught. They are working, praying, denying, affirming, con-
centrating, willing. They are in all ways building up the
perfect-idea body, transforming flesh corruptible into substance incorruptible. Thus they are following Jesus in the
regeneration. When they have renewed every organ and
every part both within and without, and have put away
all evidences of old age, the world at large will begin to
accept their claims as true: that the destiny of all men is
to transform the body of flesh into a body of Spirit and
thus immortalize it. In this manner death is to be overcome and the earth made the dwelling place of immortal
men (MJ 173, 174).

Appearances

During the forty days following His resurrection, Jesus appeared to His followers on ten occasions. "Jesus had obtained power on the three planes

of consciousness: the spiritual, the psychical, and the material. After His resurrection He held His body on the psychical and the astral planes for forty days" (MJ 173). His resurrected body was sufficiently similar in appearance to His physical body that He was recognized by many to whom He appeared. His mission was not complete until His followers were convinced of the Resurrection. The Eleven were to continue the Christ ministry, and they had to be convinced that He still lived. But since His body had been spiritualized it was not subject to physical limitations. He could suddenly appear to people in rooms where doors were closed, and could as suddenly vanish from their sight.

In the years of their association with Jesus, the apostles had never comprehended His predictions about the Crucifixion and the Resurrection. When He came to them in His resurrected body, they remembered what He had said and at last understood Him. In the garden of Gethsemane, the apostles had been so confused and fearful that they had deserted Jesus. As a result of His appearances after the Resurrection, the loyalty and faith of the apostles were renewed and they became the leaders of a faithful and united group.

These appearances are as much a part of Jesus' life as are the three years of His ministry. They verify His claim that spiritual man is all-powerful. Like the disciples of His day, Christians throughout the ages have needed such verification. Some of His richest teaching was given between the Resurrection and the Ascension. While the Gospels give short accounts of a few of His appearances, more than half of them present facts that are vital to a person's spiritual unfoldment. These lend credence to His promise: "I am the light of the world: he that followeth me shall not walk in the darkness, but shall have the light of life" (John 8:12).

Five of Jesus' appearances were on the day of the Resurrection, (Easter Sunday), and the first of them was to Mary Magdalene.

Mary was standing without at the tomb weeping: so, as she wept, she stooped and looked into the tomb; and she beholdeth two angels in white sitting, one at the head, and one at the feet, where the body of Jesus had lain. And they say unto her, Woman, why weepest thou? She saith unto them, Because they have taken away my Lord, and I know not where they have laid him (John 20:11-13).

Mary's weeping was the human reaction of grief over the death of a loved one, and added to her grief was the fear that someone had stolen Jesus' body. The two angels represent "the positive words of life that bring spiritual powers to bear that lift the body out of matter into spirit. These two bright and shining powers are possessed of animated intelligence" (MJ 168). Jesus was standing nearby, but Mary's eyes were filled with tears and at first she did not recognize Him. When He asked why she wept, she thought He was the gardener. However, when He called her by name, she turned, knew Him, and cried, "Rabboni; which is to say, Teacher" (John 20:16).

Jesus saith unto her, Touch me not; for I am not yet ascended unto the Father: but go unto my brethren, and say to them, I ascend unto my Father and your Father, and my God and your God (John 20:17).

Why did Jesus not want Mary to touch Him? Later in the same afternoon He appeared to other women and did not object if they touched Him. It would seem that Mary was closer to Him than the others, for she had served Him continually from the time He had healed her early in His ministry. Her grief, therefore, was more poignant than theirs. Charles Fillmore gives this explanation:

The I AM is Spirit, but in order to rise into the realm of pure ideas it must not be attached to the clinging affections of the soul. . . . Jesus did not want the sorrowing Mary thought to touch Him. The spiritual mind does not grieve; it does not look to matter and the limitations of the flesh for life eternal, and it dissipates the thoughts of sorrow by a denial of their reality or power to affect the mind of the Son of God (MJ 168).

The second appearance of Jesus was to the other women who had come with Mary Magdalene to anoint His body. It probably took place in the garden of Joseph of Arimathaea, and is recorded only in the Gospel of Matthew.

And behold, Jesus met them, saying, All hail. And they came and took hold of his feet, and worshipped him. Then saith Jesus unto them, Fear not: go tell my brethren that they depart into Galilee, and there shall they see me (Matt. 28:9, 10).

As these first appearances were taking place, the guards who had fled from the tomb went to the Jewish authorities and told them of the strange happenings at the tomb. The chief priests and the elders gathered and suggested to these soldiers that they must have fallen asleep and that Jesus' disciples had stolen the body. For a soldier to sleep while on duty was a crime punishable by death, but when the Jewish leaders bribed the soldiers and promised them immunity from punishment to say that Jesus' body had been spirited away, they were glad to spread this report.

Another appearance of Jesus was to Peter. The details of it are unknown, though the visit is referred to by Luke and also by Paul (I Cor. 15:5). "The Lord is risen indeed, and hath appeared to Simon" (Luke 24:34).

On the same day toward evening, Jesus appeared to two disciples on the road to Emmaus. This is a beautiful instance of Jesus' desire to open the eyes of those who believe. The two disciples, with sad and anxious hearts, were discussing the incidents of the past two days, when a stranger joined them and asked about their distress. They were surprised that anyone who lived in Jerusalem had not heard of the crucifixion of Jesus of Nazareth, "a prophet mighty in deed and word before God and all the people" (Luke 24:19). It had been their hope that He was the long-awaited Messiah. True, the report was abroad that He had risen from the dead, but no one had seen Him. These two had not heard of His appearances to Mary Magdalene and the other women. After He reproached the two disciples for their lack of understanding and faith, the Master explained the Old Testament prophecies concerning suffering and glory that were to be experienced by the Saviour. When the three arrived at Emmaus, the disciples invited Him to share their food.

When he had sat down with them to meat, he took the bread and blessed; and breaking it he gave to them. And their eyes were opened, and they knew him; and he vanished out of their sight. And they said one to another, Was not our heart burning within us while he spake to us in the way, while he opened to us the scripture? (Luke 24:30-32.)

With all speed the two disciples returned to Jerusalem to tell the great news to the apostles. They found them and others with them, but before the two could relay their news they were greeted with the joyous tidings, "The Lord is risen indeed." Then the men from Emmaus told of their experience with the risen Saviour.

Jesus' fifth appearance was in the evening, and ten of the apostles (Thomas was not there) were together in a room in Jerusalem. The door was closed. Suddenly,

Jesus came and stood in the midst, and saith unto them, Peace *be* unto you. And when he had said this, he showed unto them his hands and his side. The disciples therefore were glad, when they saw the Lord. Jesus therefore said to them again, Peace *be* unto you: as the Father hath sent me, even so send I you. And when he had said this, he breathed on them, and saith unto them, Receive ye the Holy Spirit: whose soever sins ye forgive, they are forgiven unto them; whose soever *sins* ye retain, they are retained (John 20:19-23).

John the Baptist had baptized with water unto repentance, but he said of Jesus, "He shall baptize you in the Holy Spirit and *in* fire" (Matt. 3:11).

The Holy Ghost is the same as the Holy Spirit or Spirit of truth. When we have received a concept of the relation that we as spiritual beings have to God, the old state of thought is easily dissolved and washed away by that of which water baptism is symbolical—denial. Then there come into our mind ideas direct from the Fountainhead, and we see everything in a new light. This baptism of the Holy Spirit quickens the whole man. When the mind has received words of Truth the way is open for the healing power, which is called the Holy Spirit, or the Spirit of wholeness, to descend further into the body consciousness. This outpouring, or inpouring, of the Holy Spirit is the second baptism (MD 96).

This second baptism may be considered as the taking on of divine ideas by affirmation.

The ten apostles hastily conveyed the glad tidings of Jesus' appearance to Thomas. To him the news seemed too good to be true, and he said:

Except I shall see in his hands the print of the nails, and put my finger into the print of the nails and put my hand into his side, I will not believe (John 20:25).

A week after the Resurrection, Thomas was given the proof he required, for the eleven apostles were together on Sunday evening when Jesus appeared. He invited Thomas to see His hands, feel His side, "and be not faithless, but believing" (John 20:27). Then Thomas exclaimed, "My Lord and my God," (John 20:28) and Jesus said:

> Because thou hast seen me, thou hast believed: blessed *are* they that have not seen, and *yet* have believed (John 20:29).

Thomas represents the understanding that, in the natural man, is dubious until it is convinced by proof. Jesus respected the demand of Thomas for physical evidence and gave it to him. Nevertheless, He commended those who believe even before they see the proof. When understanding becomes spiritually quickened it is the perceptive power of the mind and develops in us "the power to use the attributes of God and to understand their place and their work in the Deity. Spiritual understanding enables the consciousness to see and to feel spiritually. Spiritual understanding gives clear insight into everything, it remolds the mentality, and inspires the will to direct, to act, and to control" *(Christ Enthroned in Man* 70).

The day of the seventh appearance of Jesus is not known. It took place early one morning at the Sea of Tiberias (Sea of Galilee), where seven of the apostles had been fishing all night. Just as day was breaking Jesus appeared on the shore. From a distance, those in the boat did not know that it was He. Calling to them, Jesus asked if they had caught any fish, and when they replied in the negative, He said:

Cast the net on the right side of the boat, and ye shall
find. They cast therefore, and now they were not able to
draw it for the multitude of fishes (John 21:6).

John was the first to recognize Jesus. "It is the
Lord," he said, and then the impetuous Peter jumped
into the sea and swam to shore. There they found
prepared a meal of fish and bread, which Jesus invited them to eat.

Man's mind is the net that catches thoughts, which are
the basis of external conditions. The sea is the mental
realm in which man exists. . . . The net of man's thought
works hard and long in the darkness of human understanding and gains but little, but once the Christ Mind
is perceived and obeyed the net is cast on the "right
side," and success follows. The "right side" is the side on
which man realizes the truth that inexhaustible resources
are always present and can be made manifest by those who
exercise their faith in that direction. . . .

The bread and fish that Jesus provided on the shore
represent the supply of Spirit for the needs of the body.
Not only does the Father provide for man in the natural
world, as by the draught of fishes, but in the invisible
world of substance are elements that correspond to the
material things. Bread symbolizes the substance of the
omnipresent Christ body and fish the capacity of increase
that goes with it. Fish are the most prolific of all living
things and aptly exemplify the ability of increase inherent
in the Christ substance (MJ 177, 178).

After the meal Jesus addressed Peter, "Lovest
thou me more than these?" And Peter replied, "Yea,
Lord; thou knowest that I love thee." Then Jesus

said to him, "Feed my lambs" (John 21:15). Three times He asked for an acknowledgment of Peter's love, and three times Peter expressed his love. Three times Jesus commanded Peter to serve mankind. Peter had denied the Lord thrice, and Jesus gave him this opportunity to overcome his vacillating faith by affirming his devotion to Him. True faith has its roots in love for Christ and a willingness to serve Him.

Still addressing Peter, Jesus said:

When thou wast young, thou girdedst thyself, and walkedst whither thou wouldest: but when thou shalt be old, thou shalt stretch forth thy hands, and another shall gird thee, and carry thee whither thou wouldest not. Now this he spake, signifying by what manner of death he should glorify God (John 21:18, 19).

This cryptic prediction is explained by Charles Fillmore:

Faith (Peter), when it first begins to awaken to the Christ ideal, sees the unlimited possibilities that are presented in this new life; it realizes that it can bring into manifestation anything that may be desired. In its more mature state it realizes the necessity for service in a universal sense. The giving up of the personal self (with the consequent working from a universal standpoint) is the death whereby we are to glorify God. However laying hold of Spirit and its power should accompany the denial of self (MJ 179, 180).

After Jesus had given this prediction, Peter turned and saw John, who was following them. Peter had received his orders from the Master, and perhaps human curiosity assailed him, for he asked, "Lord, and what shall this man do?" Jesus' reply was a rebuke. "If I will that he tarry till I come, what *is that* to thee? follow thou me" (John 21:22). The highest duty of each of us is to follow Him. We should do our appointed work and not concern ourselves with what another does or fails to do. Our faith faculty (Peter) is inquisitive and dictatorial at times. We should put it under the dominion of the Christ, who alone knows how each faculty should function.

During the meal of fish and bread Jesus may have told His apostles about the mountain in Galilee where He would meet all who believed in Him. This was probably Mount Tabor, where more than five hundred assembled at the appointed time. The Gospels of Matthew and Mark record this meeting and the words of Jesus at this time. The accounts are different, and each gives a commission to those who love Jesus and are endeavoring to do His will and His work. (Another commission was given at the last appearance of Jesus before the Ascension and is recorded in The Acts.)

The commission according to Matthew:

Jesus came to them and spake unto them, saying, All authority hath been given unto me in heaven and on earth. Go ye therefore and make disciples of all the nations, baptizing them into the name of the Father and of the Son and of the Holy Spirit: teaching them to observe all things whatsoever I commanded you: and lo, I am with you always, even unto the end of the world (Matt. 28:18-20).

Man, functioning in his spiritual nature, asserts divine authority over all things (heaven and earth). In the consciousness of our Christ self, we are to teach His word, denying and affirming (baptizing) in the threefold nature of the Divine (Father, Son and Holy Spirit). We can do this only as we are continually aware that we labor in His name and that He is always with us.

The commission according to Mark:

And he said unto them, Go ye into all the world, and preach the gospel to the whole creation. He that believeth and is baptized shall be saved; but he that disbelieveth shall be condemned. And these signs shall accompany them that believe: in my name shall they cast out demons; they shall speak with new tongues; they shall take up serpents, and if they drink any deadly thing, it shall in no wise hurt them; they shall lay hands on the sick, and they shall recover (Mark 16:15-18).

The followers of Jesus are to tell the good news of the indwelling Christ to all ("the whole creation"). Those who have ears to hear Truth shall be saved from mortal limitations, while those who close their ears must remain in subjection to the restrictions that result from error thoughts. All who believe and proclaim Truth shall have the dominion and mastery of spiritual man and be able to do the works of Jesus (cast out demons, speak with new tongues, and heal the sick).

The ninth appearance of Jesus is not recorded

in the Gospels but is alluded to in Paul's first epistle to the Corinthians: "Then he appeared to James; then to all the apostles" (I Cor. 15:7).

The last appearance was to the Eleven just before the Ascension.

And, being assembled together with them, he charged them not to depart from Jerusalem, but to wait for the promise of the Father, which, *said he,* ye heard from me: for John indeed baptized with water; but ye shall be baptized in the Holy Spirit not many days hence. They therefore, when they were come together, asked him, saying, Lord, dost thou at this time restore the kingdom to Israel? And he said unto them, It is not for you to know times or seasons which the Father hath set within his own authority. But ye shall receive power, when the Holy Spirit is come upon you: and ye shall be my witnesses both in Jerusalem, and in all Judaea and Samaria, and unto the uttermost part of the earth (Acts 1:4-8).

Here is Jesus' promise of the descent of power from on high to those who are faithful to Him. Only then can we fulfill the provisions of what is sometimes called the great commission, namely, to be His witnesses to persons everywhere. "Unto the uttermost part of the earth" means to serve to the fullest extent in speaking His word, performing His works, and declaring to all the resurrecting power of Christ.

Ascension

Jesus had purposely kept His body on the psychical and astral planes for forty days in order to be with those who were to carry on His work and to complete His instructions to them. At the end of this time He made the final step in the spiritualization of His body, and the Ascension took place.

And when he had said these things, as they were looking, he was taken up; and a cloud received him out of their sight. And while they were looking stedfastly into heaven as he went, behold two men stood by them in white apparel; who also said, Ye men of Galilee, why stand ye looking into heaven? this Jesus, who was received up from you into heaven, shall so come in like manner as ye beheld him going into heaven. Then returned they unto Jerusalem (Acts 1:9-12).

As regards the Ascension Charles Fillmore states:

Through His spiritual attainments Jesus formed a spiritual zone in the earth's mental atmosphere; His followers make connection with that zone when they pray in His "name." He stated this fact in John 14:2: "I go to prepare a place for you." Simon Peter said, "Lord, whither goest thou?" Jesus answered him, "Whither I go, thou canst not follow me now; but thou shalt follow afterwards."

When Jesus had purified His body sufficiently, He ascended into this "place" in the spiritual ethers of our planet. In our high spiritual realizations, we make temporary contact with Him and His spiritual character, represented by His "name." But we, like the apostles, are not yet able to go there and abide, because we have not overcome earthly attachments. We shall, however, attain the same freedom and spiritual power that He attained if we follow Him in the regeneration. But we should clearly understand that we cannot go to Jesus' "place" through death. We must overcome death as He did before we can be glorified with Him in the "heavens," the higher realms of the mind (JC 83, 84).

Yet even before we make the final attainment, we may walk in the footsteps of Jesus. This is possible with His loving assistance for which we should ask with all the simplicity and faith of a little child. Truly,

Jesus still lives in the spiritual ethers of this world and is in constant contact with those who raise their thoughts to Him in prayer. The promise was not an idle one that He would be with those who have faith in Him. "Let not your heart be troubled, neither let it be fearful. Ye heard how I said to you, I go away, and I come unto you."

His body disappeared from our fleshly eyes because He raised it to its true place in the ether; but He can make His presence felt to anyone who looks to Him for help (JC 11, 12).

Each day presents a chance for us to go a little farther along the way that leads to eternal life. Ours is the awe and joy that was in the heart of Andrew when he exclaimed, "We have found the Messiah" (John 1:41). His words ring in the depths of our being, and we are humbly grateful to be able to accept His final commission and tell about the resurrecting power of Spirit that lifts man from the dregs of human misery to the glory of the Christ life. In many quiet meditations we catch the vision that was Paul's, and hear the words that he speaks to each one, "Christ in you, the hope of glory."

INDEX

PRINTED U.S.A.

68F-3M-2-73